W9-CNA-169

25 Biggest Mistakes Law Enforcement Officers Make And How To Avoid Them

25 Biggest Mistakes Law Enforcement Officers Make And How To Avoid Them

by

K. Karlberg

TATE PUBLISHING & Enterprises

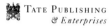
TATE PUBLISHING
& Enterprises

Tate Publishing is committed to excellence in the publishing industry. Our staff of highly trained professionals, including editors, graphic designers, and marketing personnel, work together to produce the very finest books available. The company reflects the philosophy established by the founders, based on Psalms 68:11,

"The Lord Gave The Word And Great Was The Company Of Those Who Published It."

If you would like further information, please contact us:
1.888.361.9473 | www.tatepublishing.com
Tate Publishing & Enterprises, LLC | 127 E. Trade Center Terrace
Mustang, Oklahoma 73064 USA

25 Biggest Mistakes Law Enforcement Officers Make and How To Avoid Them
Copyright © 2007 by K. Karlberg. All rights reserved.

No part of this publication may be reproduced, stored in a retrieval system or transmitted in any way by any means, electronic, mechanical, photocopy, recording or otherwise without the prior permission of the author except as provided by USA copyright law.

The opinions expressed by the author are not necessarily those of Tate Publishing, LLC.

This book is designed to provide accurate and authoritative information with regard to the subject matter covered. This information is given with the understanding that neither the author nor Tate Publishing, LLC is engaged in rendering legal, professional advice. Since the details of your situation are fact dependent, you should additionally seek the services of a competent professional.

Book design copyright © 2007 by Tate Publishing, LLC. All rights reserved.
Cover design by Chris Webb
Interior design by Lindsay B. Behrens

Published in the United States of America

ISBN: 978-1-5988688-4-5

07.10.23

Contents

Part II Problem Solve, and Persuade with a Genuine Attitude

Mistake 6 Style and Effectiveness: You're Attitude

Mistake 7 A Negotiating Behavior

Mistake 8 Mediate/Conflict Resolution

Part III Humanize Oneself

Mistake 9 Need identification

Mistake 10 Humanize Oneself Through Community Affairs

Mistake 11 Community Policing

Part IV Ethical Dilemmas

Mistake 12 Physical Aggression and Verbal Abuse

Mistake 13 Corruption

Inductive logic–Empirical data was collected, and a generalization has been developed that explains relationships between/among the subjects observed.

At certain times when interacting with individuals, why is a non-authoritarian, non-militant and nonthreatening approach more productive than traditional policing approaches?

This material has been written to enhance the productivity of Law Enforcement Officials. Our first priority is always officer safety. We have witnessed many situations in which police officers have been killed in a split second. Always proceed with caution and cater to hyper awareness while applying this material.

Comstock———- "Case Closed" People Magazine, September 11, 2006 issue of People Magazine debut the story of Detective Cheryl Comstock of the Los Angeles County sheriff's department, homicide division. "How do you catch a killer 20 years after his crime? Cheryl Comstock did it by being extra nice. Not long ago she paid a visit to Arturo J. Gutierrez, once a suspect in a late '80s murder case that had gone ice cold." "He had a dog," says Comstock, "I asked him to hold my folder while I petted the dog." "She also asked if he remembered when he'd last seen girlfriend Christie Fleming before she was found bludgeoned in her apartment in 1989. "He said multiple times that he hadn't seen her in months," says Comstock. "We just kept going over his story in a nonthreatening way." "Then she politely thanked him for his time and left."

Law enforcement officials and society have one common goal:
To thwart crime and/or interfere with its plans

Acknowledgments

I would like to acknowledge all of the individuals who supported the writing of this text book. First and foremost, I would like to acknowledge my family, Jeff and Lexy, and friends whom on a regular basis inspired me to complete these writings. My mother-in law, Dolores T. Karlberg, continuously inspired my writings and the publication of this text. In addition, I would like to acknowledge my Aunt Mary Peikert, who effectively initiated direction and advice regarding this text.

Several colleagues made respective comments on this book. I am very grateful to them for their insight. I would like to recognize my editor who worked with the manuscript before the publisher's editing phase, Lisa Ratliff-Villarreal, teaching at Colorado Technical University, San Antonio College, Cerro Coso Community College and Vincennes University. I'd like to recognize Edward Senu Oke, the head chair of the Social and Behavioral Science Department at Joliet Junior College, Joliet Illinois, who inspired my work as a writer and professor and who once told me to stay on *the right side of the road,* which I have continued to do. In addition, he wrote the foreword to this manuscript.

I'd like to thank Jay Whitney for direction pertaining to this text. I'd like to recognize Gad Bensinger (PhD), a professor in the Criminal Justice Department at Loyola University, Chicago, Illinois, for teaching me the right way during the completion of my undergraduate degree and graduate degree. I would like to recognize Robert Brown (PhD), Westwood College in Woodridge, Illinois, for always supporting me as a professor of Criminal Justice. I would like to thank Commander Samuel Cannerday from the Berwyn, Illinois Police Department, who was my very first instructor and one who guided my career in an ironic fashion. I would like to recognize Mike Casali (FIC), Bureau of Alcohol Tobacco and Firearm, for believing in me and my abilities at the federal level, and Senior Special Agent Dale Lange of Burlington Northern Santa Fe Police Department in Chicago, Illinois, for believing in my policing abilities. I cannot forget Brendan Caffrey, the best supervisor that I have ever had for his belief in my ability in the private sector.

This text is for all of my students from Joliet Junior College in Joliet, Illinois; Westwood College, including the Woodridge Campus, Illinois; Schiller Park Campus, Illinois; and Calumet City Campus, Illinois for supporting my teachings and work in the Criminal Justice Field. I would like to thank all of my students located all over the world attending Colorado Technical University online for their encouragement and support. I cannot forget Eric Jankovic, Dean of Academic Affairs (CTU), for all of his encouragement. In addition, I would like to thank my fellow law enforcement companions for guest-speaking in my classrooms and catering to my philosophy when policing.

In Loving Memory of
Dolores T. Karlberg
March 18, 1934–March 27, 2006

Foreword

As a graduate of Eastern Kentucky University College of Law Enforcement, and current chairperson of Joliet Junior College, Department of Social and Behavioral Sciences, I have had the opportunity to review many law enforcement textbooks and pertinent text materials, and I have found this textbook to be very comprehensive. In the post Rodney King era of uncertainty about the parameters of police powers, this textbook effectively speaks to the essentials of law enforcement training and the criminal justice system. The scenario-based approach of the text elucidates the practical basis of a practitioner's work, in preparing students in law enforcement programs, and criminal justice studies.

This textbook will be equally useful for students taking a course of study in criminalistics, as the text informs the psychological and sociological foundations for the study of behavioral sciences related issues. The tenor of the text is indicative of the need for a more dynamic approach to the study of law enforcement, criminal justice and the behavioral sciences. The text explicitly and implicitly shows that academic preparation should go beyond what is, into the realm of what every officer ought to know, and should know to meet changing demands. Parts I and II of the text focus on communicational training and problem solving attitudes that are essential in law enforcement officers' interaction with members of the public. The textbook shows that, effective law enforcement officers must by necessity and training be well versed in using the least volatile methods of their training to diffuse tense situations. The textbook shows that, officers who possess appropriate persuasive and communications skill are better equipped to temper the outward manifestation of human thoughts and emotions when assessing potential levels of dangerousness.

Parts III and IV of this textbook address the public engagement function of law enforcement, as a way of resensitizing law enforcement training and criminal justice studies to the efficacy of human relations function. This textbook reflects on ways to gear the mind of the officer to the notion of power distribution, when engaged in fact finding and investigatory practices. Equally, the scenarios dealing with community policing, and ethical dilemmas such as abuse of power and corruption bring to mind issues of negative public perception of the police, and how public trust can be regained. Part III and IV reinforce the fundamental imperative of training officers in the tenets of the bill of rights with emphasis on the fourth amendment guarantees for suspects and accused persons.

Part V informs the theoretical basis for attention to the adaptive and coping temperament that law enforcement officers need to imbibe, not only as professionals, but also as human beings who have relationships with significant others. The materials covered in Part V of the textbook are invaluable in the educational preparation of a balanced law enforcement officer, whose ethical responsibility is to protect the public interest, including balancing the pressures of home and work. The textbook brings to mind that all positive human attributions begin at the domestic front, and invariably, the scenario on partner communication speaks to why work related stressors must not be allowed to interfere with home life. The textbook speaks to why law enforcement training must be wholesome, holistic, and never conducted in a vacuum. Most importantly, the textbook informs the theory that best practices in law enforcement training, must be an inclusive enterprise, which highlights the importance of domestic relations, and the good life of the officer's immediate family. I believe this textbook is a must read for every law enforcement officer, and for all students that plan to pursue a professional career in the field of law enforcement.

Edward O. Senu-Oke, Chairperson
Department of Social & Behavioral Sciences
Joliet Junior College, Joliet, Illinois

Part I

Communicational Training
and the Lack Thereof

Mistake 1

Concerning Power and Authoritarianism

"The idea of acting morally must extend to how a company treats its employees. Rather than focusing just on what they earn, you listen to what they need. You harness their energy and opinions. You empower them. The old authoritarian mode no longer works."

Anita Roddick

Scenario 1

It is all about the power

The only reason that I decided to become a police officer is because I wanted author-ity and power. My dad always thought that he was the king of the household and constantly picked on me. I guess I showed him. Now when I see my dad, he is scared of me because I can beat him down at any time. I wear my uniform all the time to prove to my dad and all my brothers that picked on me growing up that I now have the power over everyone and can do whatever I want without addressing any consequences because I believe that I am above the law. I am a police officer.

Rx: Power associated with law enforcement is unfortunately implied. Indi-viduals that yearn for policing jobs because at sometime in their life they have been picked on have ulterior motives. Theses motives are indicative of show-offs, using the badge as a power symbol rather than one of a public servant. An "anything goes" attitude in order to prove power does not correspond with that of a serve-and-protect agenda. An officer that caters to the goal of a public servant will remember that power concerns itself with the cost of resistance, and coercing effectively will not resort to one having to use power. Behaving in a powerful manner will ultimately thwart important discourse because the agenda is stigmatized by proving that in the eyes of others, weakness is a factor. An officer needs to be able to react to subjects with use of communication and forget about an idea that power has been established because a firearm is being carried, a uniform is worn, and a badge is carried. A professional officer will always keep in mind that the job is to protect and serve, and power/authori-tarianism in most instances is rarely needed. Carl B. Klockars, in *Blue Lies and Police Placebos* (1984), examines truth in law enforcement. Klockars identifies four general types of control used by police officers: *authority, power, persuasion, and force.* The use of persuasion should be at the forefront of policing. Persua-sion, exemplified through the art of communication, can and should be used frequently. Close and Meier (1995) examine persuasion.

"Rather, persuasion actively engages resistance and seeks to overcome it by mobilizing signs, symbols, words, and arguments that induce in the mind of the person persuaded the belief that he or she ought to comply" (p. 229).

Persuasion through active communication can lead to non-resistant arrests, willful convictions, and even complete compliance.

Scenario 2
I must show off my power in a threatening sort of way

It was the fourth of July, and for the first time in years I was out partying all night. I decided to take public transportation so that I could enjoy myself and not worry about having to drive home. I was a bit obnoxious when approached by this nice police officer. We were having a calm conversation. Her tone of voice was soothing, and I no longer felt the need to continue my violent behavior. She listened to me and responded to what I had to say. Unfortunately, her supervisor walked up to us while we were speaking and decided to remind me of his power. He stated, "Hey what's going on? It is a good thing that you are talking to this officer because you know what happens when you talk to me?" I replied, "What?" The officer replied, "I'd take you to jail!" Subsequently, I felt threatened and reacted to this officer by telling him where to put it. I ended up in jail that night.

The form of discourse used by this supervisor was used to establish the idea that he was more powerful than the subject. However, this type of discourse did nothing more than enhance the subject's aggressive state of mind, present a challenge, and ultimately destroyed the composed situation. Subsequently, the offender was taken into custody. This undesirable consequence could have been avoided by continuing practical discourse with the subject. However, when the supervisor decided to intervene and insinuate that he had more power than the subject, a challenge surfaced, and subsequently a combative subject surfaced. The officer felt the need to establish power over the subject, but was it really necessary? Understanding a subject's state of mind is necessary as well as not catering to annoying triggers such as brandishing the idea that the officer has more power and authority. A professional officer would have not aggravated the situation with threatening discourse; instead, a continued pursuit of calming the individual with tactful discourse should have been noted, and thus a positive outcome would have been established. The power associated with law enforcement is also associated with authoritarianism. Both are intertwined with one another. *"I have power over you"* and/or *"I have authority over you"* seemingly are of one agenda. In fact, both have one common feature, and Close and Meier (1995) note the similarities.

> "Both are social as opposed to individual forms of dominance and control. They both depend upon persons acting in concert, sharing and coordinating meanings and actions" (p. 228).

Authoritarianism and power associated with law enforcement officials are social misconceptions that need to be rectified. Authority demands an unquestioning obedience. How can productive communication surface if an unquestioning obedience is demanded? Power is concerned with the cost of resistance. *"If I resist, what will happen?"* Both can be practiced interchangeably and abused simultaneously. *"If you move I will knock you out!"* An officer is demanding obedience, yet at the same time soliciting power. Therefore, authoritarianism and power are subject to one agenda.

> "What is known, though, is that all three major movements in the history of American police, their militarization, their professionalism, and their legalization are easily readable as direct attempts to encourage authoritative relations between police and citizens. Despite the fact that all three movements have been successful in some respects, all of them have met a peculiarly American mix of individualism, egalitarianism, and social heterogeneity fundamentally hostile to the enlargement of relations of authority"(Close, Meier, 1995).

By using active communication skills, authoritarianism and/or power should never surface. Explaining and/or reasoning for compliance will alleviate tension, and in essence, establish control for the officer over the situation while eliminating a threat and a negative perception of the officer. Authoritarian behavior related to law enforcement is not needed. So why is it implied? Our country is based on equality. Officers need to enforce the law, but not in the manner of tyranny, because being a dictator is not a deterrent. In fact, it innately challenges the other individual. Furthermore, when officers are perceived as threats, that perception, which stems from an authoritarian militant nature, means that "the game is on." The "game" is considered to be a challenge. However, when an officer is communicative, and therefore not viewed as a threat, then the challenge is invalidated, and social order is maintained.

Scenario 3
Eliminating a powerful threat

A correctional lieutenant has seen it all in the Cook County jail. The following incident is one in which a violent offender was brought to his division. This guy was bloody and would not stop fighting with everyone. In fact, he had been fighting all night with the officers that brought him into the jail. So he says to me, "When I get untied, I am going to really hurt you!" I said to him, "If that is the worst thing that happens to me today, then I will be doing good. Hey, I am just doing my job, buddy. I have a family, too." The suspect remained calm for the rest of the evening.

The officer in this scenario alleviated the threat of his presence, and subsequently the suspect remained calm for the rest of the evening. By the officer stating his job title and insinuating that if the offender did hurt him that pain would not be the worst experience thus allowed the offender to believe that the officer would not fight back and in essence is not a threat. The suspect, believing that the officer would not engage in violent conduct, in turn alleviated any threatening environment, and the suspect no longer felt the need to be defensive or obnoxious. Moreover, by the officer stating that he had a job to do allowed the offender to relate to the officer as an equal, a fellow human, and one that is simply trying to pay the bills as is every citizen's obligation. If the officer simply stated that he was just doing his job, did not ever feel like fighting, and continued to apply accommodating discourse in addition, the offender would have remained calm. The more non-threatening discourse that an officer can apply, the less likely a situation is to escalate.

However, if the officer would have replied, "Yeah? *Why don't you try it buddy!*" the offender would have become even more noxious because a challenge would have been offered. Therefore, the officer would have left the suspect with no choice but to react to his powerful challenge. A challenge becomes a game; a game takes two to play and relates to challenging discourse furthered by physical abuse, which ultimately relinquishes who is more powerful. When an officer gives into suspect/offender threatening behavior, then a game is established. If the officer did untie the individual and attempt to teach him a powerful lesson (not unlike many others have) by fighting the suspect to prove that he is and will always be the successor, then the officer has committed a crime of battery. An officer's worst case scenario is that there are video cameras in the prison that catch the officer in the act. The tape reaches the media. The officer is suspended, possibly indefinitely. To pursue this thought further, a civil law suit could be filed by the suspect alleging injuries, mental anguish, and demanding punitive and compensatory damages and from not only the officer, but the facility that hired him. If an officer decides to give into a suspect/offender threat and verbally or physically abuses the suspect/offender just to prove dominance/power, then that officer has committed a crime. Walker (1992) examines police brutality.

> Public disrespect was typically greeted by police brutality, which went unpunished. Continued use of force by the police only encouraged more public hostility. Ultimately this vicious circle led to a complete lack of public respect for police officers and a lack of professionalism in American policing (p.10).

An officer's job is to thwart violence and calm situations, not heighten them. Too many times officers get caught up in the moment, adrenalin kicks in, and a powerful surge of aggression is acted upon. Therefore, we witness cops beating suspects, television shows highlighting this behavior, and overall media frenzy blaming the police for anything and everything. Communication is the key to successful outcomes. An officer should cater to the art of communication and not verbally or physically react to suspect/offender-threatening terminology. One lapse of judgment or loss of control may cause a loss of employment and/or incarceration. Most importantly, when engaged in challenging situations, cater to discourse and in turn, the public's perception of law enforcement will bolster.

Mistake 2

Don't Hesitate to Communicate, but Proceed with Caution...

If citizens were asked what traits they felt were desirable in police officers, their responses might go something like this: "Police officers should be able to work under pressure, to accept direction, to express themselves orally and in writing. They should have self-respect and the ability to command respect from others. They should use good judgment; and they should be considerate, compassionate, dependable, enthusiastic, fair, flexible, honest, humble, industrious, intelligent, logical, motivated, neat, observant, physically fit, prompt, resourceful, self-assured, stable, tactful, warm, and willing to listen and accept change. Furthermore, with our society becoming increasingly diverse, the ideal officer would be able to police without bias or discrimination and be sensitive to the needs and concerns of various populations within a community." Unfortunately, no one has all of these traits, but the more of these traits that police officers have, the more likely they are to be effective in dealing with not only the citizens of the community, but law breakers as well (Wrobleski, Hess 2003, p. 374).

Scenario 4

Yes, speak! It is okay

There was one incident when I almost died. It was a typical loss prevention stop. At first I could not figure out how this individual was stealing. It took me quite a while to figure out her network; however, it finally hit me. I went up to the second level, where the individual exited the store. I identified myself; she looked at me as I was standing next to the upper level balcony. She continued to look at me, and then the railing to the balcony. We both knew what she was thinking. She was in position not to comply with my request to return to the store, but to throw me over the balcony. She was twice my size, and I was working alone. We paused for a long time before I realized that I should start talking. I managed to talk my way out of being launched over the balcony, but I knew that I had an even more challenging task to overcome when we arrived at the office. She was cold, angry, hateful, not remorseful, and very belligerent. I had never talked so much in my life. My goal was to allow her to see my side. Over an hour later, she spoke. Another hour later, she understood what I was doing, and as time continued to pass, I understood why she did what she did. She even shook my hand before leaving for lock up. Several months later I received a letter from her stating that I had changed her life. I broke the bad cop stereotype. For me this was a great accomplishment. I owed it all to the art of communication and understanding. I owed it all to simple human nature.

The officer in this scenario decided not to remain silent, but to apply discourse. Frequently, subjects are combative and use threatening terminology. An officer's freedom to communicate is restricted by administration and academies that have taught them. Contemporarily, officers are conditioned not to react to subject communication. In fact, the "beat" teaches one to either ignore it and/or threaten the subject with traditional discourse such as, "Shut up or you're going to jail"; "One more word and you're under arrest"; "I don't care, take it up with the courts"; and dehumanizing discourse looms large, such as not speaking to the subject but speaking to another officer in front of the subject about the subject. Do not hesitate to ask questions to find out what is going on in the offender's life at the time of arrest. Offer help if needed, whether it is a telephone call, employment guidance, or educational direction. Do not be afraid to break the bad cop stereotype. By breaking it, you are changing the public's perception of law enforcement from a negative to a genuine positive. The more talking one can participate in, the better the outcome. These are human beings with real problems, just poor direction. Communication will aid in breaking the poor perception of law enforcement officers.

We need to start over, restructuring the mindset of law enforcement officers pursuing a form of social engagement and thwart the characteristics of the authoritarian ideology currently in place. Muir (1977) writes:

> The reality and the subtle irony of being a policeman is that while he may appear to be the supreme practitioner of coercion, in fact he is the first and foremost its most frequent victim…Contrary to the more unflattering stereotypes of policeman, it is the citizen who virtually always initiates the coercive encounter. What is more, the citizen tends to enjoy certain inordinate advantages over the policeman in these transactions…the citizen is relative to the policeman, the more disposed, the more detached the nastier, and the crazier…The irony of the policeman's lot is that his authority, his status, his sense of civility, and his reasonableness impose terrible limits on his freedom to react to the extortionate practices of others (Muir, 1977: 44–45).

Remove the limits.

Scenario 5
Observational speech

At the local level of policing, it was a party gone bad because of underage drinking. We must have arrested thirty underage drinkers. We brought them to the station and began telephoning parents to pick up their children. I was honored with babysitting these thirty juveniles until their parents arrived. I sat in the room and listened for a long time. I knew that there were cameras in the station, so I was very hesitant to communicate with these individuals. They began to ask me questions, but I ignored them for as long as possible. Fortunately, I took it upon myself to break the bad cop stereotype, and I began speaking, but as little as possible. I learned so much information from these juveniles. I learned about their drug and alcohol use, where the parties are normally held, and I even learned who had drug and/or alcohol addiction problems and needed help. Of course, at this time I did not act upon any of the information for fear that I would lose my job. They left the station shouting lines like, "You're a cool cop!" and "You understand!" and "If we ever get in trouble, can we call you?" The change in attitude that I witnessed was amazing; they went from being cop haters to asking me if they could give me a telephone number. It was a huge turnaround, all due to the art of communication. Interpersonal communication is key to success in this field.

The officer in this scenario was hesitant in speaking, yet just a bit of communication led to information that could have become very valuable. The more one communicates, the more likely one is to gain vital information. The officer obviously realized that the juveniles wanted to communicate, and the officer decided to conform regardless of administrative consequences. Ultimately, a positive outcome was noted. When a professional officer makes an arrest, the suspect is asked why and how, and ultimately the truth is uncovered. While dealing with many individuals who are arrested at the local level of policing, an officer must learn how to remove the *bad cop* stigma through use of communication by simply asking questions, offering guidance, and stimulating discourse. Subsequently, a positive outcome will be noted. Reece and Brandt take note of communication breakdown (2002).

> "Communication breakdown has just about taken the place of original sin as an explanation for the ills of the world–and perhaps with good cause. As our world becomes more complex and we spend more time in organized activities, the need for interpersonal understanding has never been greater. And just as important, the cost of failure has never been higher" (p. 33).

Scenario 6

Filters an altered state of perception

A call came in that four individuals were harassing passengers. Everyone heard the call, and three officers were waiting for the alleged offender's arrival inside the facility. Having been present, a 26-year-old African American male and a 62-year-old white male veteran officer were also present. Age is important because it is a factor contributing to the changes in behavior from younger recruits to older veteran officers. The four white male suspects walked directly into the three officers. They were what society has coined skinheads with a subtitle leaning towards Sharps, but currently traditional. The seasoned officer immediately stereotyped the individuals and attacked the four individuals by threatening to remove them from the building and put them in jail. The veteran officer said, "Look at these freaks. Do you want to go to jail? I will put you in jail right now!" The four alleged offenders became angry and abusive.

The appearance of these four individuals was different. They were wearing leather clothing and chains. Their hair color ranged from pink to blue. Their shoelaces were differently colored than their shoes, and several piercings were noted. The older police officer stated as they were walking towards him, *"Look at these freaks!"* Subsequently, he began verbally attacking the individuals. If it were an ideal situation, a professional officer would have immediately removed the stereotype and/or label and stated, *"What is the problem? What happened?"*

The suspects then could explain that they had just missed their ride and were upset.

One officer could reply, *"Oh, I didn't know that you missed your ride. I thought you were angry at other individuals."*

The suspects might reply, *"We were yelling at our ride because we were angry that we missed it; we can certainly wait for another ride."*

Problem solved; the seasoned officer in the given scenario reacted to the appearance of the four suspects with an altered state of perception. Filters upon approach of any individual based on appearance will definitely provoke controversy, and if acting on filtered perceptions, the end result will be a negative one. Alleviate any type of stereotypical thoughts. Furthermore, stereotyping and/or labeling alters one's perception and leads to predisposed judgments, which filter the communication process. The seasoned officer first commented on the appearance of the individuals and subsequently assumed that they had committed a crime. He screamed, "*You're all going to jail*," before he even knew what had occurred. Therefore, a communication barrier was established, which deterred productive communication—a devastating mistake made by many police officers who unnecessarily shotgun a situation based on one looking the part and subsequently, communication breakdown indicative of a filtered state of perception occurs. Unnecessary demands and terminology are common, in turn provoking anger in suspects rather than an officer disregarding stereotypes and engaging in discourse; thus allowing for the root cause of a dilemma to surface and be corrected. Reece and Brandt examine communication filters (2002).

> "When people are influenced by one or more of these filters, their perception of the message may be totally different from what the sender was attempting to communicate. Both sender and receiver must be keenly aware of these possible distortions so that they can intercept any miscommunication" (p. 33).

One officer asked the suspects about their appearance and what it meant. They replied that on a daily basis they are harassed by the police because of the way they look; however, they are just expressing themselves in a way that appeals to them. The subjects said that they did not like the seasoned officer's approach, that they were insulted, it made them angry, and they wanted to fight back. Another officer approached and also began asking questions.

What if an officer approached you and said "What is your name, do you have drugs on you?" They replied that his attitude was poor and therefore, they would argue with him about answering his questions. Furthermore, they asked him why the first question that came out of his mouth was indicative of drugs. What if an officer approached you and said, "Do you need any assistance? Can I help? What just happened?"

We spoke with these individuals for an hour, and we learned about them, and they learned about us. We provoked discourse and gained information from the subjects. We decided to learn about the subjects rather than passing judgment based on their appearance. We learned that Skinheads and Sharps hate racial discrimination, and the only difference between them and us was simply music. There are many sender and receiver filters that interrupt communication and/or alter it.

Scenario 7
I misunderstood

I went to pick up my wife at work. She teaches college and had a late class. I arrived at the parking lot of the college and realized that I was several minutes early. I drove to the back of the parking lot and parked my car under a light because I wanted to read. An officer pulled up behind my vehicle and asked me what I was doing. I replied that I was waiting for my wife to get out of class. He then asked me why I don't go into the college and get my wife. I replied that I did not want to embarrass my wife. At that time he asked me to step out of the car and told me that he was going to search my car. Three other police vehicles arrived at the scene. I told him that he had no probable cause to search my vehicle. He then told me to immediately leave the parking lot. After class, my wife was greeted by this officer. He asked if I was her husband and reminded her of a drug charge that I had three years before I even met my wife. He explained to her that when I said that I would embarrass her, he thought I meant by causing a domestic dispute and was threatened by my appearance because I am six foot one inch and weigh two-hundred and fifty pounds. However, I meant that I was wearing shorts and a t-shirt and that I did not feel adequately dressed to enter the college.

The officer in this scenario assumed that the individual was threatening an act of domestic violence. A professional officer would have asked the subject to explain the statement, "*I will embarrass her,*" and the confusion would have been resolved.

Sender filters and Receiver filters:

    Role expectations

    Attitudes

    Language

    Emotions

    Semantics

    Perception

    Prejudice

    Stereotypes (appearance)

    Non-verbal gestures

    Race/Gender

    Labels

    (Reece, Brandt, 1995)

Communication is easily taken for granted and thought of as a simplistic task. It is assumable that a message is being understood with no need for explanation.

Furthermore, the interpretation of messages can be different, and realization of filters is necessary in that barriers become apparent. The communication process seems simple; however, recognition of sender and receiver filters that affect our communication process is needed. Learning how to become good listeners and clarification of statements need to be routinely practiced. The basic communication process involves a sender, then the message; subsequently the message is received, and feedback is awaited. There are filters that need to be avoided at any cost. Filters exist, and acknowledgment of these filters is significant. For example, if there is a language barrier, attempt to address the barrier. Filters can be devastating to communication because they can alter perception. A professional officer will block out perceptions based on appearance or attitude. Remember the old saying, "*Never judge a book by its cover.*"

Scenario 8
I knew she would cry

One of my worst experiences was when I was driving to the hospital. I was pregnant and highly emotional. I didn't feel good and was having pains in my abdomen. I saw flashing lights behind me. I had to pull over even though I needed to reach the hospital. The officer approached my vehicle. I attempted to tell him that I was sick, but he did not listen to me. By this time I felt faint and began to cry. He threw a ticket at me and stated, "Women are always crying!"

A favorite departmental story is one indicative of the female that cried that day and/or the female who offered sexual favors in exchange for not being ticketed. Thwarting gender specific stereotypes will not be an easy task. Society lives through stereotypes, labels, and discrimination. The media dictates how society should perceive other individuals. This officer obviously stereotyped and labeled the female driver. Subsequently, he expected a certain behavior. Therefore, a communication filter surfaced, and listening to the driver was not a priority. The driver could have needed an ambulance and/or a police escort to the hospital. When a subject seems disturbed, an officer has a duty to react to the disturbance, especially if illness of any sort is involved. Any filter can alter an officer's perception of the driver and subsequently interfere with proper judgment. Thus when a male officer pulls over a female driver, a gender filter could surface and/or have been predisposed. By not listening to the female driver, or maybe by listening too much, an altered state begins to take its course. Reece and Brandt (2002) reasonably identify a gender specific focus.

> This filter makes it appear that men and women are communicating through different genderlects, just as people from different cultures use different dialects. This anger and frustration can create a major filter that interferes with effective communication between genders (p. 37).

It is very difficult to remove communication filters including stereotypes and/or predispositions. However, this behavior places false judgments upon others, and the innocent can indeed look guilty in the eyes of the officer. The media dictates stereotypes and labels on television, radio, movies, and even now online. A professional officer will not cater to predisposed judgments because it interferes with performance.

Scenario 9
He was gangster

When I attend my classes, I always attempt to look the part. A conservative look is demanded at the college level. I was on my way to class for my final presentation. My presentation was about human relations in a gang setting. My presentation involved looking the part and presenting my evidence, which was collected and videotaped in the real world. I saw flashing lights behind my vehicle. I pulled off to the side of the road. The police officer did not get out of his car; in fact, he screamed at me to get out of my car and put my hands up. I looked around, and three more squad cars arrived. I started to shake and did not know what was going on. The officer had me get down on my knees before he approached me. He walked up to me and called me just another gang banger. I was trying to explain to him that I was dressed like this for school. He replied, "Yeah right, you are." He began to search my car, when I remembered what my teacher, a former police officer, told me to do. I said, "Hey, I am a student. You have no probable cause to search my car." Fortunately, the officer looked up, apologized, and told me to be on my way. Thanks, Teach!

The officer in this scenario catered to a stereotype that assumed that the individual had gang relations related to appearance. An effective officer would be cautious in any situation. However, an effective officer would not address an individual based on an offensive label. For instance, the movie *The Hurricane,* the story of Ruben Hurricane Carter, brings awareness to the stereotypical nature of society. An innocent man sat in prison for twenty-two years. Stereotyping must desist; not only in the minds of officers, but in the minds of the American people. Stereotypes are linked to role expectations, race and gender issues, and ultimately alter perception, which leads to false judgments. Role expectations are driven by the media's labeling of individuals based on speech, gender, race and appearance. The more education an officer receives, the less likely one is to cater to this type of behavior.

However, some departments only require applicants to hold a high school diploma to work on their force. Becoming learned in the field of social sciences including criminal justice is critical to becoming a successful law enforcement official. Until then, the capability of comprehending critical thinking is understandably weak. Therefore, a higher education is critical to those pursuing law enforcement positions.

A filter can thwart the process of communication because a learned expectation interferes with perception, reliance on facts, and credibility. In contemporary society, it will be difficult not to label, stereotype, expect, or judge; but in this type of field, these filters need to be abolished. An altered state of perception leads to an altered state of communication, whether receiving or sending. Reece and Meier (1995) examine the impact of communication filters.

> When people are influenced by one or more of these filters, their perception of the message may be totally different from what the sender intended to communicate. (p. 33).

Law enforcement recruits must practice techniques that are directed towards non-filtering agents rather than filtering agents, which will justifiably negate prejudice and engage effective communication. A professional officer will know after communicating in a natural state whether there is a threat present. In addition, a professional officer will allow the subject to determine his or her destiny by allowing him/her a meaningful chance to communicate and comply before catering to the use of force.

Scenario 10
What is going on?

An officer pulls over a male driver. The officer senses tension and responds to it by giving orders and yelling at the individual. What the officer does not know is that a wasp has just stung the subject in the foot, and he is having an allergic reaction to the wasp sting. The officer, in a maneuver we have all seen, rips the subject out of the car and handcuffs him until the subject calms down enough to explain. The officer is angry and frustrated, as is the subject.

This behavior is not the officer's fault. This is a learned reaction, which stems from training. A scare tactic is put into the minds of officers: *You never know what you are walking up on.* This is true. However, an officer needs to approach situations with the voice of communication and reason. Therefore, an officer will be alerted to the situation at hand and become aware of how to control the situation without leaving a negative perception of law enforcement, in turn allowing the American people to be more prone to cooperation and general openness with law enforcement officials. Emotions also filter the process of communication. Because of anger, the subject and the officer were not communicating. A professional officer would have calmed the subject down enough to indeed communicate effectively, and would have sought medical attention for the subject. The same mistake can also occur when using language and non-verbal filters. If a situation occurs where non-verbal gestures are made or a foreign language is spoken, do not hesitate to simply ask, *"Hey, what does that mean?"* or *"Please clarify!"* These statements are very effective. Reece and Brandt determine the impact of non-verbal messages.

> Nonverbal messages are messages without words or silent messages. These are the messages (other than spoken or written words) we communicate through facial expressions, voice tone, gestures, appearance, posture, and other nonverbal means. Research indicates that our nonverbal messages have much more impact than verbal messages (p. 37).

Remember, there is a capability to relate to other humans regardless of cultural and/or sub-cultural differences. These filters can be suspended by simply keeping an open mind and asking questions. Again, in regards to nonverbal filters, do not assume that they are threatening because the subject often becomes threatened or on guard around police officers. First and foremost, before acting, cater to communication.

Scenario 11
I thought I understood

My kids were playing outside while my wife and I were cooking dinner. She was cutting onions, and I was cutting the salad. My wife cut her finger. It was a bad slice, and my youngest son walked into the house. I was angry and told him, "Mommy cut her finger! Call 911." The police arrived, entered my home, and threw me up against the wall. One officer kept yelling at me, "Did you cut your wife? Answer yes or no!" The other officer who was speaking with my children stated, "He is angry. He is angry." Every time I attempted to explain what happened, he screamed "Answer yes or no!" I was handcuffed and put in the squad car until they figured out that we were just cooking dinner.

The officers in this scenario assumed that the father was angry and injured his wife. 911 calls are almost always chaotic, but remaining calm and attempting to rationalize situations is important. A professional officer would ask open-ended questions, which would reveal much more information than yes-or-no-type questions. *"Tell me what happened,"* and not, *"Did he or she strike you?"* Allow for explanatory answers, and then surmise. Emotions also filter communication. Do not take for granted that someone is angry or happy; always note a natural state, then seek the pattern of emotion. Offensive terminology could be as meaningless as, *"Why are you so mad,"* or *"You look really angry."* These statements in fact can change behavior instantaneously, most of the time to the defensive. Maybe now the person becomes angry or even violent. Sometimes what is expected can be easily nudged into becoming reality—the pinnacle of irony. A professional officer would cater to discourse that leaves openings. Ask open ended questions.

Mistake 3

Humiliation

Scenario 12
Control I believe

When I was arrested this officer called me a freak, loser, and a pot head in front of all my friends.

Scenario 13
Public humiliation

I was at a party with all my friends when the police arrived. They came to tell us to keep the music down. This one officer recognized me from the time my sister and I were fighting. He said, "Hey John, have yah beat up your sister lately?"

Scenario 14
Powerful humiliation

I was arrested at a bar for insulting the owner because he continuously watered down drinks. It began as a conversation and turned into a heated argument, and the police were called. I was with my family and friends when the police arrived. The officer did not allow me to give my side of the story. He just humiliated me in front of the entire club. He made statements such as, "Who is the tough guy now," as he grabbed my head and, "Listen up, loser. I don't care what happened. You're coming with me! Don't you have a record? I thought I arrested you just last week?"

A sub-cultural trait of law enforcement officials is the belief that humiliating a suspect will control situations. Humiliation is thought to weaken the suspect mentally, which is believed, in turn, to lesson the officer's chances of a violent outbreak and therefore create a safer encounter. However, the opposite is true. By humiliating a suspect in front of children, family members, and friends, the chances of violence is higher because an insult challenges one rather than alleviates the chance of violent behavior. Humiliation correlates with power. Power is applied in the form of humiliation to allegedly weaken a suspect's state of mind. However, this does nothing more than provoke violent behavior from the suspect. A professional officer will not cater to verbal or physical forms of humiliation. A professional officer is aware that insulting language can create negative outcomes and reemphasize negative perceptions of law enforcement.

Mistake 4

Public Perception and Fear

Scenario 15
Pull Over Already!

My husband and I were driving to the mall, and our four-year-old child was in the backseat sleeping when, all of a sudden, we noticed flashing lights behind our vehicle. My husband in his early years was a trouble-maker and has a record. He is scared to death when the police pull us over. They treat him differently because he has a record and he has been harassed and abused before by police officers. However, his glory days were fifteen years ago. He decided not to stop, and a chase was initiated. I was screaming at him to stop the vehicle, but he was so scared he would not stop the vehicle for several minutes. When he finally stopped panicking and stopped the vehicle, we were bombarded by police officers screaming and yelling at us to get out of the car. My husband did not mean to upset anyone. He was just so scared.

Scenario 16
What should I do?

I am working at a bar, and lately this one man keeps coming back to see me. He is odd and gives me the creeps. He stares at me constantly and claims that he knows everything about me. I found out that he is a homicide detective. He makes statements to me such as, "I just painted my bedroom blood red, I know everything about you!" He knew my name, where I lived, and even entered my locked car to close my sunroof while I was working. I am terrified because he has access to any and all information about me and my family. He makes it clear to me that he knows everything about me, and every time he comes in, I want to hide. I believe that he is stalking me, and there is nothing that I can do about it because he is above the law. What should I do?

The public has a very negative perception of law enforcement, and a fear factor has destroyed trust. A fear factor indicative of being caught and suffering abuse or the idea that attempting to evade an officer is not possible due to power are two misconceptions that the public holds. A professional officer would not abuse the badge in order to achieve status and/or a date. Furthermore, a professional officer would not physically or mentally abuse a subject. If such actions were reported to the chief of a department, the officer should suffer disciplinary actions.

There have been many discerning incidents involving police officers. It is not true to say that the public has lost all faith in policing, since the public never had faith in policing. As we discussed in the first chapter, the concept of policing embodies a militant and authoritarian ideology, which has bred abusive and overbearing officers.

Breaking the *bad cop* stereotype and beginning to gain citizen trust is indicative of active, genuine communication and not abusing the badge. If there is a conflict, try to coerce through communication the idea to stop and discuss the issue, and do not use the badge as an advantage tool. As taught by FTOs (field training officers), all officers have been taught not to engage in discourse with the subject, or to do so as little as possible. To say less is better, but rage in demanding compliance is an accepted practice. To the contrary, *to say more* is better, with as little rage as possible, because then the situation becomes controlled and not *us v. them,* or *police are threatening because they are above the law.* In fact, when an officer leaves the academy, the first issue that is addressed by a field training officer is the issue of forgetting everything that has been learned via the academy or educationally. Dantzker (1995) reinforces the idea that police sub-culture has established its own rules and training:

> Upon leaving the academy one of the tasks of the field training officer according to Lundman (1980), is to capitalize on the rookies' disenchantment with their training experiences and finalize the rookies' break with the academy experience. There is near consensus among social scientists who have studied police socialization that FTO's tell rookies that the academy experience is a waste of time and to forget all that crap they were told in the academy (p. 86).

A new police recruit must be willfully ready to fully employ education in response to unwarranted and ineffective FTO tactics and demands.

The sniper incidents in Washington D.C. drew attention from around the world. One morning the news radio station was shocked at the public's response. Every single call blamed the police for the sniper incidents. The radio-show hosts did nothing more than defend the police during every call that was taken. In fact, the sniper incidents became non-existent in the eyes of America when there was a police officer pictured on the front page of the paper pointing a gun at a car. The snipers even left statements blaming the police for not answering telephone calls and/or having rookie trainees answer the telephones. The talk show hosts had to stop taking callers on the radio because every caller made a negative statement geared towards law enforcement officers.

The Son of Sam Killer talks about the Virginia sniper:

> But he said he had been, feeling this person's anger and rage toward law enforcement. (Zernike, 2002, New York Times).

The public's perception of law enforcement has always been negative in fashion relating to fear and distrust of police officers. The root cause stems from corruption, power, and law enforcement's authoritarian nature. *To Protect and Serve* is an officer's goal; it is not intended to scare fellow Americans. Public perception must be bolstered, and by implementing continuous genuine communication techniques and sanctions for abusive behavior, it can be. In the eyes of the public, negative historical stigmas of law enforcement officials still vastly exist.

Mistake 5

Teamwork, but I Thought
We Were a Team?

Scenario 17
Us vs. Them

I remember when I was at the academy and my instructor continually stated, "Remember, it is us vs. them, the bad guys vs. the good guys." These statements were drilled into my head over and over again. When I finally reached the street, I couldn't help but to look at others as threats. In the back of my mind I felt as though everyone that was not wearing a uniform was my enemy and not on my team. I felt that my attitude changed towards others, especially when I conversed with others while on duty or while off duty. In addition, I felt that everyone was out to get me, and I could not understand my instructor's philosophy.

Scenario 18
Online lead

I tried so hard to become a good federal law enforcement officer. I became an expert on Online lead, a tool used for identifying suspects. It was a new computerized software program. Therefore, many of the seasoned agents were hesitant in learning how to use it. I took it upon myself to gain viable leads. I was retrieving so many that I decided to begin handing out leads to other agents. However, my generosity sparked argument and hostile attitudes. I shockingly realized that a team atmosphere was not in place. In fact, much to my chagrin, I was surrounded by a highly competitive atmosphere which catered to a "me" ideal rather than a "team" ideal.

Scenario 19
Hit and run

I witnessed an accident and decided to wait for the police to arrive on the scene so that I could elaborate on the facts of the accident. When the officer arrived, I was assisting the woman who was hit by a semi-truck that left the scene. I did manage to get the license plate number of the truck that was involved in this hit and run accident. When the officer arrived on the scene, he told me to leave. I tried to explain to him that I witnessed the accident, but he replied, "I will tell you just one more time, if you are not involved in this accident, then leave now!" I took the license plate number home with me. I thought that the officer and I were on the same team.

Scenario 20
Brotherly love

I love my brother very much, but lately he has been taking drugs. I finally figured out who was giving him the drugs. I called the police and reported the individual. I wanted to remain anonymous, but the officer told me that he would not pursue the incident unless I revealed my identification and assured me that it would be kept private. I gave him my information, but he wanted my date of birth and my address. I felt as though I was being harassed when I was only trying to help. When he found the individual that I reported, he told him that I called the police. I thought I could trust the police. I thought that we were on the same side. My brother has not spoken to me since that incident.

Scenario 21
Powerful competition

Internally, arrest quotas, ticket quotas, lack of trust, promotions based on production, production based on arrests, and overall factors complimenting competition breakdown of the law enforcement team atmosphere exist today. In addition, externally, a powerful persona indicative of curtness, shortness, authoritarianism, and overall a lack of communication is breaking down the team atmosphere associated with the police and the public.

> A. Officers must communicate to do their job effectively.
> B. Communication is part of teamwork.
> C. Officers are working for and with the public.
> D. One general goal is noted—*to stop crime*
>
> If A, B, C, and D are true, then a team atmosphere should be in place.
>
> Team–a number of persons associated in some joint action (Webster's Unabridged Dictionary of the English language, Portland house, 1996–1457).

Part of America's team is law enforcement, for all cater to one overriding goal, to stop crime and/or interfere with its plans.

So why is it that the police sub-culture is a team in and of itself? The *Us v. Them, The Art of War, and Machiavellian* attitudes still exist. For law enforcement to be effective, a unified team environment needs to be in place. Why don't citizens call in more crimes? Why don't citizens approach officers for help? Because a team atmosphere has not been established nor reinforced. Through communication, an effective team atmosphere can be established, resulting in more public trust. Maureen O'Brien (1995) examines team work.

> Until a group establishes common, shared goals, something all members will be striving to achieve, it is not a team (p. 3).

A unified team should have been a genesis in place. In pursuance of solving issues through communication and building community support, a need to initiate a team atmosphere is essential. Becoming a team will open up the floodgates of active communication between law enforcement and society. A team actively works together, communicates, and becomes unified through one common goal. Currently, a team atmosphere in accordance with the community and law enforcement is with little existence. Team-building of law enforcement officers and society needs to be influenced, and law enforcement should be initiating this process. By continuously communicating with the public and suspects, law enforcement can slowly build a team atmosphere. Evidence that a team philosophy can indeed work is nationally noted in the television show *America's Most Wanted*. The show begs Americans to aid in the capture of criminals. This show is a brilliant success because it caters to the idea of a unified team, police and the American people. More of this behavior across the board will be essential in establishing a team network and bolstering the public's perception of law enforcement.

Becoming a team player will demand the will to communicate with suspects/offenders. O'Brien (1995) analyzes conflict in a team atmosphere.

> The paralyzing effect of conflict seems to be related to the size of the conflict, and conflicts have a way of growing. The longer we try to bury them, the bigger they get. What starts off as a slight difference of opinion becomes the principle of the thing and a minor,

somewhat annoying personality trait leads to an intense dislike of the person exhibiting the trait (p. 71).

This dislikable trait, when applied to law enforcement officers, can be indicative of their authoritarian nature rather than a communicative, comforting, team-player attitude and understanding nature, which, in turn, would calm a situation and not heighten it. If a communicative approach were taken, then the goals of breaking the *bad cop* stereotype, bolstering citizen trust, establishing a team atmosphere, and thereby decreasing crime would all become effortless. By continuous positive communication by law enforcement officials directed toward the exercise of a unified team atmosphere, all of the latter mentioned goals would be achieved.

Part II

Problem Solve, and Persuade
with a Genuine Attitude

"Let us never negotiate out of fear. But let us never fear to negotiate."

John F. Kennedy

"The work of the righteousness shall be peace and the effect of righteousness, quietness, and assurance forever."

Isaiah 32:17

"We have thought of peace as passive and war as the active way of living. The opposite is true. War is not the most strenuous life. It is a kind of rest cure compared to the task of reconciling our differences. From war to peace is...from futile to the effective, from the strategic to the active, from the destructive to the creative way of life....The world will be regenerated by the people who rise above these passive ways and heroically seek, by whatever hardship, by whatever toil, the methods by which people can agree."

Mary Parker Follett

Mistake 6

Style and Effectiveness:
You're Attitude

"Peacemaking is the art and science of weaving and reweaving oneself with others into a social fabric of mutual love, respect, and concern."

Bruce A. Arrigo

Scenario 22
Traffic Stop or Bust

A woman and her seven-year-old son were heading east on Algonquin Rd. in Mt Prospect, Illinois, when she was pulled over by a police officer. The officer approached her car and insulted, "Is this your boy? It is obvious that you don't care about him. Give me your driver's license now! You are obviously trying to kill your own kid!

In scenario 22, the driver had her son in the backseat. The child began to cry as the officer screamed at his mother. The officer was attacking her parenting. Regardless the act of the offender, it is not an officer's duty to pass judgment on a suspect/offender. The woman allegedly ran a red light. Assume the driver did run a red light. Would there be grounds for an officer to approach the car and attack parenting practices? Of course it is agreeable that a risk factor was apparent, but an officer's job is to alert one of mistake and ticket accordingly or issue a warning. However, this officer decided to over step his boundary by verbally attacking the driver's parenting, which alarmed the driver even more than the thought of a ticket. The officer's comments were needless and offensive, which then led to a heated argument and an upset child.

Upon approach, a negative attitude towards a suspect/offender will do nothing more than cause confusion and argument. This approach in and of itself is an atrocity. A professional law enforcement official will not approach another individual with personal verbal attacks, an elevated voice level, and/or insinuations of bad parenting, especially in front of a child. Furthermore, this incident possibly thwarted any chance of continued reinforcement in the child's mind that police officers are genuine and trustworthy individuals.

The driver contacted the chief and filed a formal grievance against this officer. Evidently, this officer has had several complaints of the same nature and had a history of calling people *bad parents*. To further discuss this matter, the chief recommended that the officer in question apologize to the child and possibly be put on suspension. Whether an individual ran a red light or did not run a red light, the officer's insulting approach was completely incorrect, negative in effect, and disdaining in nature. Therefore, a negative outcome highlighting a heated argument, a terrified child, and a negative perception of law enforcement was reinforced.

A professional officer would have approached the vehicle, identified himself to the mother and child that was seated in the back seat, and reminded the driver that by not acknowledging traffic signals, accidents do occur. Example:

> "Hi, how are we doing today? Hi sport, my name is Officer X. Miss, did you know that accidents occur from not obeying traffic signals? Try to be a bit more careful. To make sure that you are a bit more careful, I am going to issue you a ticket. Okay, have a good day."

> Let us assume that the driver stated, *"But I did not run a red light!"*

> The reply, *"My job is to be very observant, and unfortunately, I believe differently, okay? I must do my job and issue you a ticket."*

Explanatory discourse along with courteous approaches will leave an individual speechless and bolster citizen perception of policing officials. The approach is very important and will shape genuine outcomes.

Scenario 23
Mean old cop

A student was pulled over for speeding, and he was indeed speeding. The officer approached his vehicle and the student said, "How are you?" The officer stated, "Better than you're going to be doing. Shut up and give me your license!

In scenario 23, the driver was asked if he would have still thought of the officer as a jerk if the officer would have replied that he was doing well, (instead of his snide reply) explained that the student could have caused an accident, and that fatalities occur from speeding. He replied, "No," and explained that he did not see it that way. However, when given the opportunity to see it that way, he felt differently.

Again, the officer in question approached the vehicle and catered to a disdaining comment rather than explaining his duty in a respectful and courteous manner and/or just doing his job.

Approaching a situation can be life threatening. As noted previously, too many times police officers stop a car and subsequently shots are fired. A fear factor has been instilled in the average citizen, thus upon approach respectful discourse is in dire need. Being explanatory will in turn calm a situation. Attitudes shape outcomes and processes of communication. Attitude is the most important part of the job. A bad attitude provokes negative outcomes.

Charles Swindoll is credited with saying:

> "The longer I live, the more I realize the impact of attitude on life. Attitude is more important than appearance, giftedness, or skill. For example, people who go through life with a positive mental attitude see daily obstacles as opportunities rather than road blocks and therefore, are more likely to achieve their personal and professional goals. People who filter their daily experiences through a negative attitude tend to focus on what is going wrong and find it difficult to achieve contentment or satisfaction in any aspect of their lives. It makes no difference how attractive, intelligent, or skilled they are; their attitude holds them back" (Reece and Brandt, p. 145).

A professional officer is aware that a positive attitude provokes a positive response. Reece and Brandt (2002) define attitude.

> "An attitude is a relatively strong belief or feeling toward a person, object, idea, or event. It is an emotional readiness to behave in a particular manner. Values serve as a foundation for attitudes, and attitudes serve as a foundation for behavior" (p. 145).

Scenario 24
You're under arrest

I happened to be watching a cop television show the other night and saw an officer pull over a speeding car. The suspect was standing outside of the car and cooperating. After the officer checked the suspect's license number he noticed that a warrant for the suspect was outstanding. He walked over to the suspect and stated, "You're going with me now! You're under arrest." The suspect fled, jumped over a barricade, and was injured with two broken legs.

In scenario 24 the approach should have been, *"Sir, there is a discrepancy with your license. Let us just remain calm and figure out what the issue is. We can work it out. Please come with me so that we can straighten this matter out."*

An officer must first try to alleviate the fear factor and then follow procedure. How many possible issues could be lingering in a suspect's mind? Is this officer corrupt? Is this officer going to abuse me? The media has cast a negative perception of law enforcement. The veteran officers are slowly dissipating along with their traditional attitudes, but a new generation of officers stands hated while having to correct the negative traditional stigma. By befriending the suspect, a world of information is offered that could be so beneficial in stopping crime. The approach in and of itself will be effective if it is not authoritarian or abusive in nature. A professional officer will cater to respectful discourse and maintain a positive attitude.

It is not difficult to surmise where the negative police attitude originated. A militant structure, one ready for war, is the answer. If ready for war, one is ready to *kill or be killed*. This militant ideal instills in police officers angry and even hostile attitudes. Throughout life, values are shaped by family, mentors, and peer groups. This in turn shapes attitudes, which shape behaviors. Early American policing was highly corrupt; in fact, one had to pay money to even become a police officer because it was a political position of power. Walker (1992) examines early policing.

"Officers were selected entirely on the basis of their political con-nections. In New York City, a $300.00 payment to the Tammany Hall political machine was the only requirement for appointment to the force." (p. 11).

There was no training and/or educational requirement. There was no supervision for these officers. Their job was based on politics; therefore, dis-crimination, abuse and corruption ran rampant. Citizens regarded police officers as political figures lacking in the "protect and serve" duty category.

At the beginning of the twentieth century, law enforcement went through change. This change was initiated and demanded that the quality of policing be enhanced. This is where we will note a serious mistake. August Vollmer, superintendent of the District of Columbia police force, 1898–1915, provoked this professional movement. Vollmer was responsible for a lot of positive change in policing. In fact, he began the first school that taught criminal justice. He, too, advocated higher education for police officers. The Reform Agenda had seven points to be addressed: To eliminate political influence, appointing qualified officers, catering to nonpartisan public servants, height-ening personnel standards, introducing different management styles, develop-ing different units, and the cancer that has now poisoned law enforcement officers today—military style discipline. This agenda demonstrated change and is relevant even today. Rather than appealing to the idea of a police officer acting as a public servant, we redirected its mission towards that of a paramilitary-type individual. We need to recant this practice. Contemporar-ily, it has become a practice by all law enforcement agencies, but is slowly changing. Because of the negative history that law enforcement has suffered, we now witness attitudes scorched by hate towards police officers. More-over, this militant ideal rather than that of a public servant and team player has inherently provoked negative responses from the public and shaped law enforcement's negative attitudes toward civilians while on the job. If the professionalism's agenda includes a militant ideal, then our attitudes form accordingly and establish a behavior indicative of the militant ideal.

"Police reform progressed very slowly. By 1920 only a few departments-Milwaukee, Cincinnati, and Berkley could be labeled professional. In most other cities police departments remained mired in corruption. Chicago seemed to resist all efforts at reform. Despite all failures, the reformers could claim one great success: They firmly established professionalism as an ideal, and their agenda dominated police reform for decades" (Walker).

Again in the 1960s, we noticed a reform movement. The Supreme Court became involved in police procedures and constitutional standards, including the due process of law. Regardless, police corruption still loomed large. Riots between the police and African Americans occurred almost every day. Shootings of African Americans became a common practice. A new age of reform began, and along with it many organizations were formed in the areas of research, law enforcement education programs, police foundations and crime commissions, and overall personnel practices were restructured. Today, we are still facing old problems, just new agendas. We now battle gang violence and terrorism. We need an even newer agenda.

"In the first problem orientated police experiment, officers in Newport News, Virginia, attacked crime in a deteriorated housing project by helping the residents organize to improve the project itself" (Walker).

A reshape of our policing agenda is at hand, and by reshaping our agenda targeting a public service platform will establish effectiveness, and gain public trust. This ideal not only shape's attitude, but will shape the attitude of society. The history of policing will make it very difficult to reshape the attitudes of the public. However, our attitudes toward the job need to dismiss curtness, disdain, and authoritarian/militant behaviors. Attitudes should reflect a willfulness to help others as a public servant, a mentor, mediator, problem solver and/or manager. Our attitudes need to become positive and not negative. *Have you ever heard a police officer say, "How can I feel positive after a day is over because I deal with negativity everyday" The job does not have to be negative. Why not ask yourself at the end of your shift how many people you helped today? How many problems did you solve? Did your positive attitude rub off on any one else? Did your positive attitude affect others?* Maintain a positive attitude when dealing with others. Try smiling when you are asked a question, or respond to one. History has shaped the attitudes of the police in an incorrect fashion. A need to change the focus and establish a more serviceable attitude is at hand. A need to dismiss the ideal of a militant attitude and focus on one of a public servant has become a necessity and will be much more effective.

Mistake 7

A Negotiating Behavior

"This mistake is dedicated to all the law enforcement officers who continuously deal with conflict on a daily basis. These individuals are committed to resolving issues, mediating disturbances, and working accordingly with the public. An officer needs to find solutions to problems without creating more conflict. By appealing to the authoritarian method, we create more unnecessary conflict. We need to improve our negotiation strategies and include analysis of individual behavior. The methods in which law enforcement approaches, communicates, and resolves issues with society should be of a negotiating behavior."

Karlberg

Scenario 25
Do not fear to negotiate

You approach a drug sale in progress. The money is in sight, and the drugs are switching hands. Both individuals are arrested. The Miranda rights have been read. You are at the station, and interrogation begins. You have a hunch about the big boss and need a name. Instead of threatening, yelling, and invoking fear in the suspect, why not sit down and begin talking about drug overdoses of teenagers, drug related shootings, and sight other examples? Then ask for help, ask why, ask how, be friendly, be a good listener, personalize a story about yourself, understand, ask questions, make sure that the individual is told that he or she is doing the right thing. Act in a way of aiding and not threatening. The answers one needs will be given with names and valid addresses.

Scenario 26
I like my music loud!

I like my music loud, but my neighbors don't and they always call the police. The police routinely come to my door, knock, tell me to turn off my music, and leave. One day a police officer came over, asked me about my music, when I play it, and told me that she would be back in a minute. When she came back she told me that the neighbors will allow me to play my music anytime Friday or Saturday, but not on Monday and Wednesday from 5:00 p.m. to 9:30 p.m. I agreed—problem solved." Thanks, officer!

Scenario 27
Halloween

Known offenders tend to repeat the same offenses on the night of Halloween. Parents allow their children to stay out late at night. Children egg houses and harass other kids. Even when they get caught, they never get in trouble because police officials just call their parents to pick them up. However, this year was different. As an officer, I decided to visit a known offender's home before the night of Halloween and requested to negotiate a trade-off. If this repeat juvenile offender gets caught again this year egging houses and beating up children, he will have to clean up the neighborhood dog feces during the winter months. However, if the repeat offender does not egg houses and beat up other children this Halloween, he will not have to clean up dog feces this winter. The offender decided not to egg houses and harass other children this Halloween. Know your community.

Dog's barking, kids fighting, friends quarreling, neighbors disputing, and general negotiation exists in the day and life of an officer. Negotiation is highlighted in law schools, but severely neglected in police academies. This is a learned process and relates to service in a different fashion. The power of negotiation is critical in police work. Fisher, Ury, and Patton (1991) examine negotiation.

> "How one negotiates and how one prepares to negotiate can make an enormous difference, whatever the relative strengths of each party" (p, 3).

The ability to persuade someone to do or not to do something is the art of negotiation.

> "If you understand the other side and they understand you; if emotions are acknowledged and people are treated with respect even when they disagree; if there is clear two-way communication with good listening; and if people problems are dealt with directly, not by demanding or offering concessions on substance, negotiations are likely to be smoother and more successful for both parties" (p. 6).

Recall the citizen fear factor previously identified by using the technique of negotiation. Fisher, Ury and Patton (1991), claim that negotiation can eliminate the fear factor and enhance citizen trust.

> "A message does not have to be unequivocal to be clear and effective. In many cases, helping the other side understand your thinking-even when you are of two minds about something-can reduce fears, clear up misconceptions, and promote joint problem solving" (p. 4).

If an officer approaches a situation and begins to ask questions and subsequently listens attentively, the situation does not become challenging for the suspect nor does the thought of rebellion because a negotiating philosophy promotes a less threatening atmosphere. This philosophy is emphasized by Fisher, Ury, and Patton (1991).

> "Showing that you have heard the other side also increases your ability to persuade them. When the other side feels heard by you, they are more apt to listen to you. Once the other side knows that you understand what they have said, they cannot dismiss your disagreement as simple lack of understanding" (p. 7).

Service can be applied in understanding how to negotiate effectively rather than power applied in a physical manner. Influencing the individual through negotiation techniques is a key factor in becoming a successful police officer. The worst-case scenario is when a suspect becomes non-compliant and will not cooperate in the negotiation process; subsequently, the use of force must surface. Simple techniques such as sympathizing with the suspect and/or negotiating peaceful resolutions will help in obtaining more information than the technique of authoritarianism and/or threatening for compliance. In addition, a negotiating behavior will create a positive perception of law enforcement officials.

At this time, outcomes should not be focused on; however, the process of negotiation should be examined. Outcomes mean finished; however, processes are ongoing, with the potential of being finished. Cooperative negotiation tactics can resolve issues and bolster citizen trust. A study conducted by Gerald R. Williams (1993) concluded and agreed that non-combative negotiators will be successful.

> "We received a total of 351 completed questionnaires, giving us that number of very richly detailed descriptions of negotiations who were considered effective by their peers. In our review of the literature, we had hypothesized that the results would show that cooperative approaches to negotiation were more effective than tough or combative approaches" (p, 157).

The cooperative style negotiator is an effective negotiator, and Williams (1993) has developed traits that pertain to this type of negotiator: trustworthy, ethical, fair, courteous, personable, sociable friendly, gentle, obliging, patient, forgiving, intelligent, dignified, and self-controlled (p. 160). Working towards genuine outcomes will not be difficult if a cooperative personality is at the forefront of an officer's agenda. Williams (1993) claims a win–win negotiating technique is possible.

> "Cooperatives are quintessential win–win negotiators. On the other hand, effective aggressive negotiators see it completely differently. Their attitude is this, if all you want me to do is go around making everybody feel good about themselves, you don't need me....It's not worth getting up in the morning for; it's not a serious objective. So they are win–lose negotiators; they want a clear winner and a clear loser; if the score is still tied, then the game's not over yet; you have to go into overtime" (p. 161).

In the criminal justice field, the cooperative approach works best; however, catering to the aggressive approach in some instances might be necessary, but just save it as a last resort. Simply allow the subject to choose his or her destiny by giving him or her an initial chance of a peaceful resolution. Williams claims that 99 percent of the time, a cooperative approach is effective and an aggressive approach is ineffective.

> "One reason that ineffective aggressive negotiators are so obnoxious or irritating is that they make unreasonable opening demands or offers" (p.163).

Demanding upon approach leaves an individual angry and in turn can cause severe negative consequences. Proceed with caution when catering to an aggressive approach because firearms are easily accessible to the public, and retaliation might surface. Williams (1993) establishes objectives of a cooperative negotiator, and they are as follows:

> "If I am fair and trustworthy; If I make unilateral concessions; Then the other side will feel an irresistible moral obligation to reciprocate" (p.167). A professional officer will cater to a cooperative negotiating style approach.

Mistake 8

Mediate/Conflict Resolution

"We see ever increasing urgency in mediating, cutting across, and reducing these imbalances for the very sake of human survival."

Bruce A. Arrigo

"Mediation requires listening emphatically and respectfully to the power holders' response and ultimately listening most carefully and respectfully to one's harshest or most immediate critics. As one learns what the opposing parties' interests are, one's own direct and vicarious experience of choice(s), when discussed in relationship to the choices of others, can assist the conflicting parties in developing a repertoire of options."

Bruce A. Arrigo

Scenario 28
Cheerleading

It was the night of cheerleading practice. A call came in from the local school that parent's were fighting at the school. I arrived at the scene to find five sets of parents standing inside the school, outside of the gym, and they were heckling the coach and participants. Some of the parents' children were former participants but were dismissed from the team for various violations. The team was a very competitive team that competed nationally. Therefore the stakes were high. I sensed jealousy, outrage, and hostile attitudes. I told everyone to leave immediately or they would be arrested.

Instead, if the officer would have stood patiently listening for a short period of time to the parents venting their frustration about the team and certain student participants subsequently, explained to the parents that by acting in such a way in front of fifty young children that their behavior was negatively affecting the children and that a more appropriate time and place for conflict resolution should be established, a positive perception of the officer and a less hostile environment would have been noted. Furthermore, if the officer would have elected a credible parent to coordinate a time and place for a mediation process, in which the officer was free to assist a peaceful resolution could have been established.

Scenario 29
Rake your own leaves

A call came in that neighbors were disputing. One neighbor claimed that the other neighbor continuously threw leaves into his yard instead of bagging them himself. Both parties were older and very angry. The receiver of the leaves insisted that the leaf-thrower should be arrested for trespassing and littering. After speaking to the leaf-thrower, I realized that due to his age, it was too difficult for him to bag all the leaves in his yard and, therefore, simply tossing them into his next door neighbor's yard was a healthier option. I told the leaf-thrower to stop throwing leaves into the neighbor's yard or he would be arrested.

Instead, if the officer would have explained to the receiving party that the elderly man had health issues and simply could not bag his own leaves, requested that the receiver allow the thrower to set a can by the side of his fence on the day of leaf raking possibly allowing the elderly gentleman to put his leaves into the can rather than in the receiver's yard would most likely have solved the dilemma. In addition, if the officer requested a favor of the receiver, such as tying the knot on the bag and setting it over the fence for the elderly man so that he could dispose of it, the issue could have been resolved.

Scenario 30
Paint ball

It is summer time, and all the kids are out of school. A call came in that a child was rapidly firing a gun that was spraying some sort of paint all over the caller's home. When I arrived on the scene, I saw pink paint everywhere, including splattered on the house of the caller. A young boy just received a gift from his aunt, a paintball gun. I confiscated the paint ball gun.

A productive outcome would have been established if instead, the officer would have asked the child to clean the paint off the elderly lady's home and apologize to her. To enhance officer perception, one could have suggested that the child set up a target surrounded by wooden boards and plastic, rather than target practicing on houses.

Furthermore, if the officer explained the danger of paintballs, reemphasized protective gear, and spoke to the parents about supervision in that only target shooting in a designated secured protected area should be allowed, it would have reinforced a peaceful resolution. In addition, the officer could have suggested a contract between the parents and child stipulating the aforementioned requirements, which would have allowed the continued use of the paint ball gun if obeyed.

Scenario 31
Spanish Lesson

Today I was a mediator. I was on duty when a man came running down the escalator yelling at me. This gentleman proceeded to tell me that he was upstairs in the restaurant and that a couple of Hispanic employees were badmouthing him in Spanish. What the employees did not know was that the individual was Cuban, and therefore, spoke fluent Spanish. I cannot even repeat what he allegedly stated. It was so shocking that I was at a loss of words, and the only thing I could say to this tourist was that I was sorry. I calmed the tourist down and walked him upstairs, wrote down the name of the employee in question, took down the supervisor's phone number and location and gave the information to the tourist. When it was all said and done he looked at me and said in broken English, "Thank you, I liked the way you handled this." I told the workers in Spanish that many people speak Spanish and to be very careful what they say when others are present! They apologized to the tourist.

Sometimes a law enforcement officer becomes a mediator in which he or she must mediate conflict between individuals. When a call comes in for a dispute between neighbors or between spouses, it's those dreadful calls that suggest high probabilities of violence. However, there are methods that will help resolve the tension between parties. Law enforcement officers make choices and possess discretion in implementing solvable alternatives. Police officers need to be able to mediate conflict and apply decision-making techniques. Police officers need to be able to implement alternatives and solutions that can create remedies for disputes. Harris (1990) suggests that a peaceful person that caters to peaceful rhetoric motivates peaceful resolutions.

> "Such a disposition would orient a person towards caring for others, using compassion, respecting diversity, seeking non-violent alternatives, and mediating conflicts" (p. 255).

Police officers need to peacefully cater to conflict resolution.

Conflict resolution involves mediating disputes, which requires a level-headed officer, one that maintains control, and one that can reasonably analyze situations. A professional officer will deescalate a situation rather than escalate a situation. Peaceful rhetoric is effective in these tense situations. Furthermore, conflict can lead to violent outcomes.

Arrigo (1999) reemphasizes the growing concern pertaining to conflict resolution in the criminal justice field.

> "We are only too aware of the escalating nature of violence in domestic situations, in street corner encounters, with police-citizen transactions, with guard-prisoner exchanges, with prisoner-prisoner encounters, and generally with various interactions citizens have with criminal justice system and its operatives" (p.211).

Police officers deal with violent situations on a daily basis. Police officers need to utilize language that promotes peace, which will deescalate situations and provide for non-violent outcomes. Arrigo (1999) examines the deescalation of violence in the butterfly catastrophe model applied to peace making.

> "It is time to explore the possibilities of applying the butterfly catastrophe model to methods of decreasing interpersonal violence. This will be an important addition for those who have focused on conflict regulation, mediation, and resolution" (p.204–205).

The butterfly catastrophe is assisted by the cusp catastrophe; concentration on the butterfly catastrophe highlighting the pocket of compromise will be examined. Application of the butterfly catastrophe provides suggestions of peaceful rhetoric that can deescalate conflict and produce nonviolent situations. The butterfly factor is indicative of peaceful discourse. For instance, Arrigo (1999) explains that if discourse relating to restricting a subject's outlet (example: *you are under arrest*), is at hand, it limits the subject's options and subsequently a violent attack would have a high probability of occurring (p. 213). On the other hand, when an individual feels that he or she has alternatives of escaping, then violence would be less likely to occur (See scenario #24). Katz (1988) has shown that uncontrolled emotions can lead to rage and violent attacks. The works of Katz (1988), Matza (1969), and others "*indicate that a certain moment in the escalation process, the person finds him-or herself more*

object than subject. Creating time intervals or time lags may provide the pause or space
necessary for returning the pacified subject to a reclaimed active position of agent"

(Arrigo, 1999 p. 220). Arrigo (1996) emphasizes that discourse can produce behavioral effects. *"In other words, when a person speaks, she or he takes up*
temporary residence in a language system that ensures the relative stability of that
grammar and that discourse's limited meanings. Discourse, in this view, is performative:
it produces effects in behavior" (Lee, 1990), speaking through the subject (Arrigo,
1996 p.214) and speaking the subject (Milovanovic, 1996). Arrigo (1999) suggests a peace rhetoric. Harris (1990) also suggests peaceful rhetoric.

> "As he indicates, such as disposition would orient a person towards
> caring for others, using compassion, respecting diversity, seeking
> non-violent alternatives, and mediating conflicts" (p. 255).

Furthermore Harris (1988) *"peace, a concept which motivates the imagination*
......implies human beings working together to resolve conflicts, respect standards of
justice, satisfy basic needs, and honor human rights" (p. 7). In simplifying the butterfly catastrophe, the divergence of peaceful discourse must surface when
catering to mediation, conflict resolution, negotiation, and overall discourse.
As stated previously, when a subject feels that limitations are being enforced,
a negative outcome is highly probable. When less perceived limitations exist,
a less likely chance of a negative outcome is probable. Where limitations
accompanied by mirrored discourse occur, violence is more likely. However,
when fewer restrictions are placed on the subject, along with subsequent
peaceful rhetoric, a negative outcome is less likely to occur. Arrigo (1999)
highlights the fact that the pocket of compromise has not reached a place of
stability, and the pocket may quickly close. However, if given the chance, an
officer should rip the pocket of compromise open by perpetuating peaceful
rhetoric. Arrigo (1999) claims that even though chances of irritation might
occur, there is a less likelihood of violence occurring. However, the peace
rhetoric is still having some effect in producing agitation (highly probable)
rather than violence (less probable) (p. 219). Peaceful discourse as reinforced
in previous chapters can deescalate conflicting situations. A professional officer will cater to peaceful rhetoric rather that authoritarian/threatening discourse when mediating and resolving conflict.

Once an officer resolves the conflict and implements a solution, an officer must be able to act upon his or her decision.

> "To look is one thing. To see what you are looking at is another. To really understand what you see is a third. To learn from what you understand is something else again. But to act on what you have learned is all that truly matters" -LeBoeuf, (1985).

Therefore, officers must have choices and alternatives and possess the behavior and discretion to act upon said decisions. More (1984) examines the act of decision-making.

> "While all of us make variety of personal decisions, only about 10 percent of the members of any organized work group have the ability and the desire to exercise formal decision making authority" (p, 289).

There is an obvious lack of specification in this area, which in turn produces ambiguity and vagueness and becomes an enigma for law enforcement officers. Decision-making policies in regard to mediating conflict resolution should be implemented and customized by a degree model. We need creative individuals that can mediate and resolve conflict, persuade, and negotiate. In addition, the implementation of critical reasoning, mediation, and negotiation techniques needs to be introduced into academies. The position of police officer should not belong to the high school graduate because one does not properly learn how to critically evaluate until a higher learning experience is exhausted. Police leadership officials need to trust scholarly officers with decision-making, mediation, and conflict resolution techniques. Furthermore, administration should not advocate limited speech, use of force, authoritarianism, and curtness. The internal police administration needs to allow officers the discretion in making choices. Internal factors need to:

1. Specify goals and missions

2. Allow for discretion to aid officers in feeling comfortable in carrying out their duties

3. Initiate a higher level of autonomy

4. Give leeway regarding departmental policies and regulations (ticket quotas)

5. Make resources available to aid officers in obtaining information on decision-making regarding precedent

6. Require more education, which will limit needless and traditional training efforts

7. Find academies that cater to reasoning, communication, decision-making, conflict resolution, and negotiation techniques

8. Revamp award system to honor those for decision-making, negotiation, mediation, and conflict resolution techniques. Instead of how many arrests the officer made this month, reward for how many incidents he or she resolved

9. Request detailed reports of how the officer deterred the crime or negotiated a peaceful resolution

10. Create a non-authoritarian officer and a team player

All of these factors will aid in changing the steel tone of law enforcement to a more peaceful one, which in turn will bring a new world of information to the officer, enhance citizen perception, and create a safer environment. Mediation/conflict resolution requires identifying the problem, creating solutions to those problems, and implementing the best solution to resolve the problem. Thus, mediation/conflict resolution consists of:

1. Identification of the existing problem

2. Creating the solution

3. Accessing the solution

4. Reevaluating the solution

5. The capability to act on the solution

6. Accomplishing the solution

7. Accepting negative feedback

8. Adjusting the solution (if needed)

The SARA model is also helpful to officers during problem solving dilemmas. The SARA model highlights four strategies: 1) Scanning–examining groups of incidents and identifying the problems; 2) Analyzing–keeping your data and collecting data from all sources; 3) Responding–implement the solutions, and; 4) evaluating your solutions.

Simple creative solutions enforced by law enforcement can enhance citizen perception and create an amicable environment. A professional officer will verbally establish relationships with other human beings by creating solutions to their disputes. A professional officer will become an advisor, mediator, negotiator, and a problem-solver.

Part III

Humanize Oneself

"An officer is not above the law and must approach tasks in a natural state rather than a powerful state."

Karlberg

"Man is the only animal that can remain on friendly terms with the victims he intends to eat until he eats them."

Samuel Butler

"Man is a rational animal who always loses his temper when he is called upon to act in accordance with the dictates of reason."

Oscar Wilde

Mistake 9

Need identification

Scenario 32
I was robbed

We were being robbed. I woke up to see my husband face down from a blow to the head. I dialed 911, the robber fled, but my husband was severely injured. I was hysterical. When the officer arrived on the scene, he told me to get back, stay away, and knock it off. The ambulance arrived. I left with the ambulance for the hospital. I received not one comforting word from that officer.

Scenario 33
I need my insulin

I was leaving Carson Pirie Scott when a loss prevention agent approached me and asked me to return to the store with him. I did so. He accused me of shoplifting and was reviewing a tape when I alerted him that I was diabetic and needed my insulin injection. He ignored me. I repeatedly requested that my hand cuffs be removed so that I could administer the injection. I sat for an hour begging for my shot. I eventually lapsed into seizure and woke up in the hospital. Thank you for the one million dollar settlement!

Humanize means to make human and/or personal. The question: How can we productively interact with others while maintaining a natural state? A natural state is neither aggressive nor passive it is natural state of awareness directed towards the other individual's persona. There are four components to humanizing oneself: improving interpersonal communication (which was addressed in Part I); identifying needs of others; being ethical in nature, which we will discuss in Part IV; and learning that my attitude will shape outcomes (Part II).

If a police officer is in the mist of an encounter, he or she must address, if necessary, the need of a subject. Every person has a need, and if one can identify another's need, subsequent positive outcomes will be established. Furthermore, by identifying a need, a happier and more cooperative suspect will be noted. The sniper incidents in Washington DC were devastating to society. Psychologists were interviewed, and questions pertaining to why someone would want to randomly kill Americans were posed. Psychologists stated that this sniper probably was withdrawn, had a family crisis in his or her life, had a dark side, or someone did not notice that something in this person's life had gone severely wrong. Identifying the needs of others creates a motivational force indicative of cooperation. Abraham Maslow (1943) argued that all individuals have needs, including physical and psychological, which affect their behavior. There are five basic needs that Maslow identified. Police officers need to be concerned with two types of needs—higher order needs and physical needs. Higher order needs consist of prestige, recognition, self-image, self-confidence, self-worth, belonging, esteem, self-actualization, and any individual behavioral need. Physical needs for our purpose are indicative of medical attention and/or illness. Tosi, Rizzo, and Carroll (1986) conclude "*that there is empirical support for need theory and, in particular, Maslow's conceptualization of need theory*" (p.221). A police officer as a human being has a duty to interact with other human beings and, in stressful situations, has a duty to appeal to comfort. A professional officer will begin identifying the needs of subjects/offenders during the initial interaction, and by doing so, a motivated cooperative environment will be created. A professional officer will suggest guidance whether it relates to medical attention, shelter, food, drug treatment programs, employment, rehabilitation facilitation, health and human services, and/or departments of child welfare. A professional officer will not hesitate to assist a fellow citizen, regardless of the need. A professional officer will take the time to identify the needs of a victim, suspect, and/or offender. In turn, this leaves the subject with a genuine impression of law enforcement, which bolsters public perception. Identifying the need and catering to the need in turn bolsters the subject's motivation, denoting that someone cares about the subject (that in itself could be the need), which leaves the subject motivated to do the right thing. A professional officer will not disregard an emotional victim, an injured suspect, and/or an offender who needs medication or guidance.

Mistake 10

Humanize Oneself Through
Community Affairs

Scenario 34
Friend or enemy?

I was assigned to work the Labor Day community picnic. As a new recruit, I stood and observed seasoned officers' work. I noticed that they stood guarded from the community. They looked mean and remote and did not speak to the members of the community. When someone would ask them a question they would reply, Do I look like the information desk?

Scenario 35
The carnival

It was summertime, and all the carnivals were planned. I was assigned to work the local carnival for the weekend. Many officers stood in a circle and talked all night. I decided to meet the community, walked around, found trouble, and expressed concern. I found out that Saturday a fight was planned. I found out that the carnival workers were exposing themselves to children in the outhouses, and discovered that the more individuals that I spoke to, the more information I gained.

In this scenario, the officers that stood in a corner all night and chose not to humanize themselves failed in the social aspect of their position. The officer that decided to cross the line, so to speak, gained valuable information by interacting with the members of the community. An officer should always want to be aware of his or her surroundings and speak to as many individuals as possible. Hyper awareness, which will be discussed in the second edition of this text, is a necessity to survival for any law enforcement official. When speaking, kindness accompanied by respectful discourse is important. A professional officer will not alienate himself from the community but will interact with the public when any opportunity arises. Thus, the public reacts positively and feels comfortable in relinquishing information. Life-saving information could be gained by just maintaining a hyper aware persona, which couples engagement in everyday dialog with members of the community.

Mistake 11

Community Policing

Scenario 36

Community policing or window dressing

I remember as a new recruit delivering flyers every summer to each house in the entire city. It was an extra assignment that was paid to us by some type of grant. The flyers were indicative of a survey about the actions of the police in the community. This assignment was titled Community Policing. When we retrieved the flyers, any negative flyers about other officers were thrown into the garbage can. In fact, one citizen asked me to write down on the flyer a personal complaint about an officer. When I finished, my sergeant directed me to throw the complaint away.

Community policing, a term that is vague in description yet contemporarily active in many different forms, is common jargon in every department. In fact, definitions range in philosophy from proactive to reactive indicative of the community. Ideally, community policing should encase community relationships with the police, such as the idea of block captains, community watch programs, and an overall agenda of service for the citizens of the community. Community policing and its meaning depends on the department's implementation of the concept. Some departments claim that they have created a community policing plan, but this is only a window dressing used for gaining grant awards. Community policing should be linked to a relationship with its citizens on a personal level. A professional law enforcement agency is aware that closer involvement with the public should be established through community policing. Furthermore, a professional agency realizes that a community policing window dressing in exchange for grant funds does not enhance citizen–police relationships and fails in pursuit of bolstering citizen perception of police officers.

Part IV

Ethical Dilemmas

A component to productive police work is to always act in an ethical manner. Morals, values, and ethics are an enigma to most. Some common questions regarding ethics are "How are they acquired?" and "What do they mean?" What is it to do the right thing, act in the right way, and act in an ethical manner? These seemingly difficult questions can be answered by applying Immanuel Kant's categorical imperative:

"To always act in such a way that the maxim of my action can and will be made a universal law."

Immanuel Kant

"Certain qualities are imperative for entry-level police officers, such as honesty, ethics and moral character. Nowicki identifies 12 traits of highly effective police officers: enthusiasm, good communication skills, good judgment, sense of humor, creative, self-motivated, knows the job and the system, self-confidence, courage, understand discretion, tenacious, and have a thirst for knowledge." (Nowicki, 1999, pp.45–46)

Mistake 12

Physical Aggression and Verbal Abuse

Scenario 37
Lessons with punch

"Repeating itself............................. I was hit, I was pushed, I was shoved, he dug his knee into my back, he twisted my arm until it was black, he punched me in the face, he sprayed my body with mace, he kicked me twice, he beat me with his asp I cried, He banged my head into the car, he tightened the cuffs where blood ran far, he blackened my body, he spit in my eye, she held me while he screamed your mine now sucker! I wanted to die!"

"The officers at the scene exercised excessive force in order to secure the compliance of the driver, Rodney King. However, much to the chagrin of the officers George Holliday was able to capture the incident on tape. King was repeatedly beaten by several police officers" (1991).

"Abner Louima was arrested during a fight outside of a New York nightclub. He was taken to the 70th precinct. Officer Volpe sodomized Louima with a broom stick" (1997).

Scenario 38
Irritation

I was chased down the street for walking on some old guy's grass. An officer who hit me with his asp and shoved me to the ground caught me. He would not allow me to get up until I promised that I would never walk on that old man's grass again.

Scenario 39
Um good

I was arrested for public intoxication. I was thrown onto the street and handcuffed as my face was buried in the gravel. I could not breathe because I had a mouth full of dirt and gravel. The officer made me swallow it.

Scenario 40
We got your number

I was fighting at a bar, but I did not start it. My girlfriend initiated the fight, and I had to protect her. I was taken to the station and every officer on duty that night attacked me verbally and physically. I was on death row for a while for a crime that I did not commit. I was released and found innocent. However, my name is muddied, and they knew it. They called me scumbag, gang banger, and told me to stay out of their town. They spit on me in the station, kept pushing my head against the wall, and ultimately held me for two days with no charges.

Scenario 41
The bully

My friends and I are underage but always buy beer and cigarettes. This one cop tracks us down every Friday night. He throws me out of the way and steals our cigarettes and beer. He calls me a loser, and dirtball in front of all my friends. He grabs my hand and squeezes it until I begin to cry in front of my friends, then he punches me one last time and leaves the scene.

Contemporarily, police brutality and verbal abuse are not accepted law enforcement practices. Police officers have a tendency to be fashionably rough. Mainly, the academy is responsible for this practice because a fear factor is highlighted when teaching arrest tactics. In addition, many times an officer can walk into a situation and immediately lose his or her life. An officer does not want to be injured and therefore is taught to approach a situation with aggressive behavior. However, in certain instances, this behavior can escalate once one becomes caught up in the moment, an adrenalin rush becomes overwhelming, and a surge of aggression takes control of the officer. A professional officer will refrain from verbal abuse and/or physical aggression. Moreover, an officer will practice methods that will maintain control over one's physical being. Falling captive to an intense urge to punish by means of force and abuse is not an accepted practice of law enforcement. Close and Meier (1995) identify in Carl B. Klockars: "*Blue Lies and Police Placebos*" the ends of force:

"The domination and control force seeks is physical" (p. 229).

As one is aware, the courts are responsible for punishment. Polluck (1998) explains why police through use of force attempt to sanction.

"For instance, police may feel that use of force in some situations results in quick justice that the courts are unable to deliver" (p. 150).

Officers have the ability to use force, and sometimes that force is abused. Furthermore, when the use of force is abused and publicized, its negative effect is reinforced to the public. Kerstetter (1985) says:

"...the appropriate use of coercive force is the central problem of contemporary police misconduct. Indeed we would go further, to argue that the history of policing has been characterized by a dynamic search for the means by which to optimize the use of legitimate force: utilizing it as necessary to maintain order, but not to the extent that it is excessive and abusive" (p. 149).

The term *force* inherently provokes fear, which correlates with the negative public perception that currently resides in the minds of the public. Dempsey (1999) is concerned with the negative public perception of law enforcement.

"Nothing undermines public confidence in the police and in the process of criminal justice more than the illegal acts of police officers." (p. 296).

Furthermore, police brutality has devastated citizen/officer relations.

Contemporarily, verbal abuse is not an uncommon practice. Derogatory terminology can be linked to the *us. v. them* mentality. Walker (1992) identifies this dilemma.

"Derogatory terms are often an expression of the general alienation of police officers from the public. In specific situations, officers use them as a control technique: to establish their authority by humiliating or demeaning the citizen." (p. 234).

In common, racial slurs, insulting language, threatening language, and overall curtness are routinely practiced by law enforcement officials. Walker (1992) found that the offensive language used by police officers occurs quite often.

> "Observations of police at work have found that offensive labels for people are a regular part of the working language of police officers. Reiss found that 75% of all the officers observed used some racially offensive terms" (p. 234).

A professional officer will apply genuine communication methods, which will create genuine productivity, control situations, alleviate tension, and establish positive outcomes.

Verbal abuse is contemporarily more prevalent than physical abuse. Dempsey (1999) suggests an advancement of verbal abuse.

> "Despite the high incidence of headlines about police brutality, evidence suggests that the verbal abuse of citizens by officers is a more serious problem."

Dempsey (1999) also took note of Albert J. Reiss, Jr. study that was conducted relative to police abuse, and the study identified the most common complaints about police officers:

> "Use of profane and abusive language, use of commands, stop and frisk violations, threatening force, brandishing a night stick or pistol, and use of physical force" (p.303).

A professional officer will not cater to verbal or physical abuse in any situation.

Mistake 13

Corruption

Scenario 42
Overall theft

Wallets, money, lighters, cigarettes, knives, pocket change, fireworks, beer, bottles of booze, and all small collectables are confiscated by police officers every day. Subsequently, and supposedly put into lock-up? Where? Do we have a room for that stuff? Oh I didn't know.

Scenario 43
It's all about me, man!

Kickbacks, bribes, favors, gratuities, theft, Fourth Amendment violations, shakedowns, smack-downs, and abusive crack-downs all in pursuit of personal gain epitomizing corruption. Hey man, count me in!

Scenario 44
No one will know

It was a routine search warrant. I was present along with three other officers. Another officer and I entered the premises and began our search. I noticed an open safe in the wall. We opened the safe and found twenty-five thousand dollars cash inside. I went to get a baggy to put the money in, and when I returned the money was gone. When I asked the other officer about it, he claimed that he never saw any money. He repeated this claim several times in front of the other officers. I knew that he took the money.

Scenario 45
Boom Boom!

It was the night of the fireworks show. As a rookie officer, I observed and stood guard on the outer perimeter of the display. At the end of the night my lieutenant called me over to his vehicle. He opened his trunk and said, surprise! There must have been five thousand different fireworks in his trunk. He told me to pick one, anything I wanted. Of course, I did.

Scenario 46
Sneaky

We made a routine arrest on a Friday night. When my field-training officer frisked the individual, he found two knives, one switch blade, and a lighter. He put all four items into his pocket, and we never spoke of it again.

Scenario 47
The Categorical Imperative

You are chasing two subjects that have just stole a pair of sunglasses from a department store and have already run one mile, you are becoming angrier and angrier because you are tired. You become frustrated, weak, and disgusted. Finally you catch up to the petty offenders. They are laughing at you! Did you decide to strike one of them? Grab one of them and throw the subject forcefully to the floor? Maybe elbow one of them in the nose? Hopefully if you chose the latter, it was caught on tape! I got it! Charge the subjects with a felony rather than a misdemeanor. In fact, the crime no longer regards one pair of sunglasses worth $100.00; it now will involves factiously $1000.00 worth of merchandise. That will teach them to steal and then make you run two miles.

> "Now you must recall the imperative and consider the situation. The subjects were probably scared. They might have been scared of what you might do to them. They might be thinking about the forthcoming wrath of their parents. It's possible that they never intended to steal, in fact it might have been a dare and juveniles love dares.
>
> Now put yourself in their position; how would you want to be treated by the police if you were in this situation? More importantly, however you react can and should be made a universal law."

Corruption in law enforcement still vastly exists. Whether stealing on a search warrant, frisking a subject and taking personal items, searching a vehicle without probable cause, accepting gratuities in exchange for favors, or routinely shaking down juveniles for packs of cigarettes, corruption surrounding officers is widespread. Corruption can be rectified by an applicable moral philosophy. Morals, values, and ethics can become a personal enigma. What it is to do the right thing, act in the right way, and be able to decide what is good versus what is bad are difficult questions to answer. Immanuel Kant's categorical imperative will aid in answering these questions:

> "To always act in such a way that the maxim of my action can and will be made a universal law" –Immanuel Kant

Having ethics means having a set of moral principals, morals meaning a right moral conduct. It is time to critically analyze what is right and what is wrong. By following Kant's categorical imperative, one should be aware of what is right and what is wrong. First, clarification of Kant's philosophy is needed. In addition to following Kant's imperative, background information for evaluation purposes is necessary. Kant believes that human beings have a duty to act in a right way and to act in a right way towards other human beings and, furthermore, that human life is the pinnacle of intrinsic worth. Immanuel Kant regards human life as an end and not as a means to an end. In contemporary society we continuously use individuals as a means to an end. Sometimes we have good reason to do so. For instance, when a subject is interrogated concerning information relating to a crime or in regards to relinquishing information about another individual, the subject is being used as a means to an end. The means-to-an-end philosophy also concerns utilitarianism, the greatest good for the greatest number principle, which Kant strongly opposes. If, for instance, a plane carrying two-hundred people is overtaken by terrorists and is on its way to crash into the Sears Tower, but the United States shot it down, this concept would relate to using the individuals on the plane as a means to an end and in summation the greatest good for the greatest number principle is achieved. The means being that the two-hundred lives on the plane were sacrificed and the end being that we saved two-thousand possibly awaiting death due to a crash into the Sears tower. In summation, the greatest good for the greatest number principal was a success. The categorical imperative incorporates an implied conformity rule. If the action should be made a universal law, subsequent conformity is demanded. Kant's categorical imperative can be used as an algorithm and, if followed, can clarify instances of uncertainty in that an established applicable method for determining ethical certainty will be secured. "*If I claimed revenge by brutally beating suspects, would I want that practice to be made a universal law?*" "*If I became a corrupt law enforcement officer, would I want every officer to follow suit?*" "*If I stole on search warrants, would I want everyone to be a thief?*" "*If I sexually harassed someone, would I want everyone to be acting as such?*" "*If I searched vehicles with no probable cause, would I want that practice to be a universal law?*" Why not, because it might happen to you? A set of ethical and/or moral standards personally relating to the professional officer are in need. One must have a disciplined philosophy to apply in times of uncertainty. More importantly, capability of acting subsequent to application should be routinely emphasized. If we as law enforcement officials constantly remind ourselves of the categorical imperative, subsequently we will become better human beings and better law enforcement officers.

Mistake 14

Gratuities

Scenario 48
Great dog gratuity

Barney at Red Hot Dogs gives you a free lunch everyday, and you graciously accept the lunch and thank Barney. It is Friday night when a call comes in from Barney's home; it is a domestic call from his wife. She claims that Barney attacked her, blackened her eye, and pushed her down the stairs. Now everyday for two years you have received a free lunch from Barney's restaurant. Barney has become your good friend.

Scenario 49
The favor

Routinely you stop at the 7–11 where all uniformed officer's drink free. The owner, Jay, has become your very good friend. In fact, you converse with him about an hour every night while you drink your free Pepsi and eat a few free doughnuts. One night Jay asks you for a favor. He tells you about a civil problem he has with an old friend. He bought a motorcycle from this guy a year ago, but the guy never gave him the title. He now needs the title fast because he now wants to sell the bike. He wants you to go to the old friend's house in uniform, retrieve the title, and scare him a bit. You explain to Jay that this is a civil matter now; it is not in your scope of duty and that you would need a warrant to go into the guy's house and take papers. Jay does not care about your excuses, and he reminds you of your free food and drink that you have taken every night for a year. He emphasizes that he really needs this favor!

Scenario 50
Lock and load

Working as a police officer demands time spent at the range. Firearm qualification and practice is required. Therefore, range time is imperative. The range master becomes your friend. In fact, he does not even charge you for range time anymore. When you run out of agency ammunition, he offers you free ammunition. You take it and have a blast. One Saturday afternoon, you are indulged in semi-rapid fire when you notice your friend, the range master, teaching his children and their friends how to shoot a 9mm Sig Sauer and 357 Smith and Wesson. He motions for you to come over and asks if you, a police officer, will teach his oldest daughter, who is seventeen, how to shoot? The state that you live in requires one to be of a certain age and possess a license to shoot a firearm.

Scenario 51
Beef and cheddar

The local fast food joint gives free beef and cheddars to all on-duty officers. When one is in uniform, the local fast food joint is the place to be! While you are eating your dinner, the manager screams at an employee and throws a cup of ice, which hits the employee in the face. She stands asking you, what are you going to do about this?

Scenario 52
Nickels and dimes investigator frenzy

You are working as a private investigator for a licensed company. Your next-door neighbor sends over food approximately four times per week. You befriend your neighbor. Even though you tell her not to send over food, you anxiously await the arrival and are eating great. She asks for a favor. Her sister believes that her husband is committing infidelity and asks you to independently investigate. However, you must be licensed in the state that you live in to practice independently. You inform your neighbor that for liability reasons you must work under your company and subsequently, provide her with information on how to contact your company to initiate the investigation. Your neighbor insists that she does not want to go through your company and offers to slip you money on the side for your work. You inform your neighbor that you cannot help her. She telephones you the next day and asks that if she was to call your company and request you to investigate will you only bill the company for one hour of work and any other time you spend she will pay you under the table?

There are ethical concerns relating to the acceptance of gratuities. Gratuity means the acceptance of a favor in exchange for some type of act. However, a police officer at the time of the act does not identify nor expect the end to the gratuity. Gratuities in any form—liquor, magazines, candy, soda, coffee, food, money, discounts, and gifts—are easily offered and easily accepted. If an officer is doing a job as everyone else on a routine daily basis, then why is the officer offered infringements? Miller and Hess (2002) identify the inequality and code of silence practiced by law enforcement.

> "A belief that officers are above the law, coupled with the code of silence previously discussed can leave officers in ethical dilemmas. A study by the National Institute of Justice, The Measurement of Police Integrity, surveyed 3,235 officers from 30 departments and found that the majority of respondents would not report a fellow officer for accepting gifts, meals or discounts, or for having a minor traffic accident while under the influence of alcohol" (p. 47).

A professional officer will exemplify a zero-tolerance policy on gratuities. The categorical imperative would have denoted not to accept free lunches because if everyone did, then capitalism would not exist and Barney would be out of business. Instead, the officer chose to accept the food and now feels a duty towards Barney. A bias and a communication filter become apparent. Therefore, the situation may be handled differently than a similar situation. Ethics and morals in policing are spoken of, written about, and a formalized manual of standards is handed out. However, a method for application has not been prescribed. Learning how to respond to unethical situations and how to apply an ethical standard will be an easy task if the categorical imperative becomes principle.

Mistake 15

Fourth Amendment Violations

"The right of the people to be secure in their persons, houses, papers, and effects, against unreasonable searches and seizures, shall not be violated, and no warrants shall issue but upon probable cause, supported by oath or affirmation, and particularly describing the place to be searched, and the persons or things to be seized."

Fourth Amendment to the United States Constitution

Scenario 53
I was ready this time

Every time I get pulled over, an officer tells me to get out of the car and searches my vehicle. This time I was ready. I arrived home late from school. I live in a semi-bad area so I wanted to park my car across the street in another parking lot. I parked my car and got out of my car when I heard a voice say, Get over here. There was a police car, and sitting in it was a police officer. He asked me to go get my license and bring it to his car. I did; he looked at my license and then looked at me and said, I am going to search your car now. Luckily, I had just left class and our topic was privacy highlighting Fourth Amendment violations. I looked him in the eye and said, Officer there is no need for that, what probable cause do you have? He replied, You're right, have a good night and sped fast away! I never knew what probable cause was. I shared my experience with the class the next week. Thanks, Teach!

Scenario 54
Probable cause, duh

"Shawnee Davis, an Olympic speed skater now represented by the NAACP, *is suing the Chicago police department for an illegal search of his vehicle." (NBC news, March 24, 2003).*

Beck v. Ohio, 1964: "The officer testified that he heard that Beck had a bad reputation, was a gambler, and memorized his appearance. Beck was arrested and searched. Rumors regarding reputation do not constitute probable cause."

Scenario 55
Privacy not illegal embarrassment

I pulled into a dark alley and parked my car. My girlfriend and I wanted some privacy. Along came the police. They demanded that we both get out of the car, and they searched the car as we stood on the side of the road. They opened the glove box and took a pack of gum, my cigarettes, and a pen-like flashlight and then made me open my trunk.

Contemporarily, stories of Fourth Amendment violations are overwhelming. The media highlights Fourth Amendment violations, and most citizens do not understand that probable cause is a required element to search a vehicle. A warrant needs to be obtained to search a place, and a full search of a person is only applicable if a suspect is arrested. A professional officer is aware that an illegal search and subsequent seizure of evidence can dismantle an entire case. Furthermore, an illegal search can result in civil liability, criminal prosecution, and enhance the negative perception of law enforcement that is persistently instilled in society. A professional officer will justifiably and cautiously conduct a search of a vehicle only when probable cause exists (Carroll v. United States, 1925), consent is given (Schneckloth v. Bustamonte, 1973), an arrest is made of a person (Washington v. Chrisman, 1982).

To react to probable cause, a belief must be substantiated by facts that a crime has been committed, a crime is in progress, or a person has been arrested. Mere suspicion is unwarranted, evidence is in demand, and generally notable only in the case of arrest. Siegel (1997) defines probable cause.

> "Probable cause to search a place and seize evidence consists of facts that would lead a prudent person to believe that items sought are sizeable items (i.e., contraband, the fruits of a crime, instrumentalities used to commit a crime, or evidence of criminality) that are or soon will be located at a particular place" (p. 197).

However, three high profile exceptions to probable cause exist. There are other exceptions to probable cause, which we will not be highlighting: inventory, border, good faith, patriot act, etc...but let's focus on the following three high profile exceptions: plain view (*Harris v. United States, Arizona v. Hicks,* (1987)), open field (*Oliver v. United States,* (1984)), and consent to search.

Plain view: If a vehicle is pulled over for speeding and a firearm or drugs, for instance, are placed in the front seat of the vehicle within plain view of the officer, subsequently, a search can be initiated.

Open field: If a plane is flying over an open field and drugs are seen as being produced, again a search can be conducted.

Consent: If an officer asks an individual if he or she can conduct a search and the individual gives his or her consent, then a search can be conducted.

A professional officer is aware that a traffic ticket does not warrant probable cause to search a vehicle and that a warrant is required upon entrance of a home. Entering a home without a search warrant will result in excluding any evidence collected from the home for trial (Boyd v. United States, (1886) Weeks v. United States, (1914), Mapp v. Ohio, (1961). We refer to this as the exclusionary rule, which has thought to have been a deterrent for police officers. Justice Blackman reviewed the Oaks research and other studies conducted on the deterrent effect and decided that there is *"no conclusive evidence that the rule has or does not have a deterrent effect. The fruits of the poisonous tree doctrine* (Silverthorne Lumber, 1920 (exclusionary rule) *becomes a cost/benefit procedure for police officers."* If beneficial means can be produced from violating an individuals 4th amendment rights, for instance, the end result being that the evidence might be included in court rather than excluded, an officer ponders; is the illegal risk worth taking? An officer consistently applying the categorical imperative to situations will coun-teract illegal practices. Critical reasoning by an officer pursuing ethical standards before acting illegally should be practiced routinely, respectfully, and considered the end of genuine police work.

Mistake 16

Lying and Policing an Accepted Practice

Scenario 56
The cabana boy

I was living in my parent's cabana in the backyard. At approximately 7:30 a.m., I heard pounding on my cabana door. It was the police. They told me to get out and that they were going to search the cabana. I did not know that they could not search my cabana without a search warrant. I told them that I did not want them to search the cabana. They stated that without a warrant they could search not only the cabana, but my parents' house, too. They did not have a search warrant. Lesson learned.

Scenario 57
But my parents

I was told that if I gave up the name of my friend I would get to go home. The officers kept repeating, just tell us everything that happened and you won't get in trouble.

Scenario 58
Huh, immunity

If you turn in all your drug connections, we will see to it that you receive immunity. They promised me, so I cooperated. Then, after I relinquished all the names they needed, an officer said, welcome to your new life as a prisoner!

Scenario 59
Subject preparation

I work for the railroad. I was caught stealing items from the cars when they arrived at the station. I know that I was wrong for doing so and felt terrible. When the officer's questioned me, I was very cooperative. In fact, the one officer simply told me to do the right thing, so I did. The supervising officer yelled at me, threatening that if I am not cooperative I will go to jail, but if I am, I will not go to jail. I had already decided to cooperate and do the right thing. Finally, I asked if I returned the merchandise if I would get to keep my job. The one officer said to do the right thing and that she was not sure about me keeping my job. I decided to give the items that I stole back, anyway.

However, the supervising officer kept repeating, "Fine. Don't worry. You can keep your job." Immediately I was fired.

Lying in policing is a generally accepted practice by law enforcement officials, courts, and society. The lies told in the process of conducting criminal investigation and questioning suspects are two common situations in which the immorality of lying is negated. Most commonly, lying occurs when attempting to obtain confessions. All in the good nature of utilitarianism. However, a dichotomy must be recognized acknowledging the difference in police classifications. An undercover officer is left with no choice but to lie. An undercover officer might have to pretend to be someone that he or she is not, and therefore, lying becomes a necessity. More importantly, for the officer it becomes a safety issue. Differentiation of an undercover officer and a uniformed officer must be established. A uniformed officer has no reason to pursue the art of deceit. An undercover officer pursuing a crime engulfed in a fictitious situation for safety reasons is left with no choice but to lie. An arresting officer must be distinguished from an undercover officer and thereby, for sake of argument, focus in this segment is particular to a uniformed police officer.

A uniformed officer's deceitful tactics should be limited. A uniformed police officer lies so that a rapid effect can be established. For instance, in the cabana boy scenario, the police did not want to put forth the required effort of obtaining a search warrant. Therefore, they decided to take advantage of a naive suspect and in turn, achieved a timely effect. In the case of questioning suspects whereby fraudulent promises are agreed upon again, less effort is noted because more information is relinquished in an accelerated manner. Carl B. Klockars (1984) examines Blue Lies in policing.

> "Thus, in the police officer's view, to lie when one can achieve
> the same effect more efficiently and with less effort is not immoral
> but stupid" (pp. 531).

However, a change should be subject to this practice. Professional uniformed officers will rely on the art of communication and persuasion rather than justifying lying applied for the sake of an immediate end. In addition, during the interrogation process, instead of threatening a subject with jail time, why not explain behaviorally that doing the right thing is important? Coercion and persuasion should hold precedent over scare tactics and lying. Explaining to the suspect his or her rights, obligations, and consequences should be the agenda, not making false promises or catering to threatening terminology. Individuals that have had negative experiences with law enforcement officials have been lied to at one time or another and/or have taken note of trickery and verbally abusive tactics. A proper interrogation can produce unlimited amounts of information by simply proposing a cost/benefit profile highlighting character benefits rather than acting with fraudulent and/or abusive intent. A professional officer will retain a search warrant prior to entering a home; will not search a vehicle without probable cause; will not seek fraud or verbal threats as an ally, but will cater to honest communication that in turn will achieve successful and fruitful outcomes while bolstering citizen trust.

Mistake 17

Stop and Frisk

Scenario 60
What the heck?

Every time I walk down the street this officer stops me, pats me down, and then insists that I come with him to his squad car where he questions me for an hour. I am a law abiding citizen.

Scenario 61
Casual conversation

My friends and I always stand on the corner talking. Every night the same officer shakes us down. We even have to take everything out of our pockets and purses. He takes money and anything of value. We are not doing anything wrong; we are just talking.

Scenario 62
Engagement party

I went out late one night to a jewelry store. I was planning to ask my girlfriend to marry me. I was looking through the window of the jewelry store at the wedding rings. I had to go out late because we both work days and I had to wait until she was asleep. I spotted the perfect ring, when all of a sudden I heard a voice say, "Don't move." A police officer was standing behind me. I attempted to explain that I was looking for a wedding ring, but he did not listen. He searched my person and walked me back to my car and searched my car, too. Do we not have any privacy?

Scenario 63
Graham v. Conner (1989)

"Graham, a diabetic, was having a sugar attack. He asked his friend to drive him to the store for some orange juice. When he arrived at the store he felt that the line was too long. So he ran out of the store to go to another store hoping for a shorter line. Officer Conner saw Graham speedily leave the store and followed. Officer Conner decided to make an investigatory stop. Graham's friend told Officer Conner that Graham was suffering from a diabetic attack. Officer Conner called for back up when Graham fell to the ground. Back up arrived, and one officer hand cuffed Graham while ignoring the friend's statements that Graham was sick. The

officers then carried Graham over to the squad and placed him face down on the hood of the car. Graham asked the officer to check his wallet for his diabetic card. The officer told him to shut up. Graham suffered a broken foot, a bruised forehead, wrist injuries, shoulder injuries, and a permanent loud ringing in his ear."

The court ruled that the officers did not use excessive force during this investigative stop. U.S.C. (1983)

The stop-and-frisk law arose during the case of Terry v. Ohio (1968). Police officers historically and routinely stopped and frisked individuals. Contemporarily, police departments warn officers to limit this exercise because of liability. A *Terry* stop can become a dangerous game. If an officer abuses *Terry,* a series of consequences can follow. Violating any portion of the *Terry* doctrine can result in criminal action, civil action, and disciplinary action. Modernly, police officers are taking advantage of discretion when initiating a *Terry stop. Terry* is at times being used as a scapegoat, resulting in intrusions to privacy in violation of the Fourth Amendment. A professional officer will be aware of the standards involved and act accordingly. Reasonable suspicion is a vague term in definition and has given justification to police officers in stopping a person. Reasonable suspicion can lead to a Terry stop and frisk. Reasonable suspicion justifies a brief stop of a suspect for identification questioning and patting the suspect down. A brief stop is key to completing *Terry* successfully (United States v. Sharpe (1985). In scenario 60, the officer did not act briefly. A safe *Terry* stop would be indicative of an officer noticing or based on hearsay (extended Adams v. Williams, (1972) a bulge in the pants of a suspect and stopping the suspect for a brief pat down and/or as extended in *Adams* the officer may reach into the clothing of a suspect when seeking a weapon. The *Terry* rule has been extended to anonymous tips (Alabama v. White, (1990).

The courts have clarified a structure for reasonable suspicion in United States v. Cortez (1981). The totality of the circumstances must be taken into account. The totality of the circumstances must in all cases contain two focuses: there must be probabilities derived from information regarding a person. Furthermore, the suspicion must involve the assumption that the individual being stopped is involved in wrongdoing. Thus both focuses must be present before reasonable suspicion is founded.

Many extensions of the *Terry* rule have surfaced. The *Terry* doctrine is vague and risky. An officer should have a clear understanding of the limits that *Terry* poses and react accordingly. A professional officer will become informed on all applicable extensions indicative of *Terry* before exercising it and always pursue *Terry* with ethical regard.

Mistake 18

Inappropriate Discretion

Scenario 64
Happy birthday

It was my twenty-first birthday. It also was my golden birthday. My friends and I were out drinking all night. We left the bar with a bottle of champagne in the car, and the radio was cranked up high. I was driving. I remember flashing lights behind us. I pulled into a parking lot. The officer approached the vehicle and asked me to step out of the car. He issued a sobriety test. I was having a good time performing it! I asked him if I was to give him a kiss would he let me off.

We drove home drunk that night, and I never received a DUI. It was a great birthday.

Scenario 65
Puppies for sale

My husband and I decided to have a litter of puppies. English Mastiffs are rare dogs, and at the time everyone wanted one. After the puppies were born, my husband took six weeks off of work to care for the newborns because I was a student and had to attend classes. I interviewed several potential canine caregivers, and then we made our final decision. A police officer really wanted a puppy for his fiancé. I was hesitant in selling puppies to unmarried couples for stability reasons. I set all of my fears aside and sold the puppy to the officer. I stipulated in writing that no returns would be honored. Three months later the officer called, wanted to return the puppy, and wanted his money back. His fiancé and he had broken up. I had conversed with this officer, and he knew that I was a student in the town that he patrolled. I refused to give him his money back. Every night thereafter when I attended school, I received a parking ticket. I had been given twenty-five tickets by the time I gave in and took the puppy back. Regardless, if my meter read two-hours or fifteen minutes, I was issued tickets.

Scenario 66
I'm a cop

I know because I am a police officer that I will never receive a speeding ticket, for that matter I will never receive any type of ticket. In fact, I was caught spying on my ex-girlfriend, but the cops that caught me at the scene knew that I was a cop, and therefore, nothing ever happens to me. Hey, we take care of our own.

Scenario 67
Blow horn

My friend and I were driving by a police officer who had a car pulled off to the side of the road. I had a blow horn and as we drove by the officer, I blew the horn at him. Shortly thereafter, we were pulled over by this same officer who cited us for four violations and continued to repeat, "Let me find another one.

Discretion is a vital law enforcement tool. However, discretion must be used ethically. In instances that involve corruption, gratuities, and bribes, officers tend to lose sight of genuine discretion techniques. The officer has the means to choose alternatives and determine outcomes. These processes must contain an ethical element; otherwise, discretion can become an avenue towards unlawful events.

Since the age of the *Bobbies,* Police officers in many instances hold power of discretion. Regardless of the limitations that administration attempts to implement, discretion still is an active part of the profession. An officer's ethical inherence will determine ethical use of discretion or unethical use of discretion. Discretion is needed in law enforcement. The application of discretion sometimes is gullible to unethical behavior. For instance, the birthday scenario is unethical because the officer accepted a promiscuous act in return for not issuing a ticket. Either preference or a type of gratuity can muddy an officer's discretion. Showing preferences or accepting gratuities in exchange for some amount of discretion is unethical. Wrobleski and Hess (2003) examine preferences correlated with use of police discretion.

"Some male traffic officers, for example, are known to issue warnings to females who violate laws and to issue tickets to males for the same violation" (p. 334).

Allowing officers discretion allows officers the power to cater to unethical discretion. Many types of filters can poison ethical discretion, such as discrimination, prejudice, gender, bribes, stereotyping, racism, and bias. Polluck (1998) determines that discretion can create unethical instances.

"However, this opens the door for unethical decisions. The power to make a decision regarding arrest creates the power to make that decision using unethical criteria, such as a bribe in return for not arresting" (p.152).

The officer must always cater to genuine ethics when applying discretion in situations. The categorical imperative would not have elicited a kiss in exchange for not being ticketed because sexual gratuities in exchange for freedom would not make for a genuine universal law.

In the puppy scenario, an officer possessed a vendetta against the individual and therefore abused his ticket-writing discretion. The officer maintained the idea that he is above the law and made it clear that challenging the officer would do nothing more than continue the antagonistic harassment of parking tickets. Police officers are given a packet of tickets in hopes that usage will be of an appropriate nature and abuse will not surface. This constitutes discretion because the ability to write a ticket or not write a ticket can lead to abuse of discretion as understood in scenario # 65. Abusing ticket-writing privileges because an officer has the means to do so or using the ticket as a coercive tool to achieve cooperation, pay-backs, or bribes is unethical. The categorical imperative would not warrant ticket writing used as a tool in exchange for a desired end. This would not make for a genuine universal law.

Overall discretion allows an officer to not issue a ticket, not make an arrest, distinguish charges, bias report writing, determine the onset of guilt, and /or simply allow a suspect to leave without being charged. An officer on a daily basis decides the fate of individuals and with that can abuse discretion. Furthermore, if the suspect is a law enforcement officer, then often no violation is issued because in the mind of the officer, he does not want to experience the same treatment. Ethics in discretion can keep an officer honest or lead the officer into the black hole of corruption. The categorical imperative applied to discretion can save an officer from liability and criminal action.

Scenario 68
Leads computer

When I was 18 years old, I was living in West Chicago, Illinois. At that time it was known for gang violence. I had a lot of friends who were connected to gangs, although I was never in a gang. My friends and I were driving to the store one day when we were pulled over by the police. The officer took my name and date of birth. Today I am 27 years old and was pulled over just last week. The officer screamed for me to exit my car, lie on the ground, and put my hands behind my back. When the officer approached me, he picked me up and threw me against the car. I was in shock. I found out that on the Leads computer from nine years ago it read, Gang Relations. How do I get that off my record?

Contemporarily, in almost every squad car, officer's have access to suspect/offender records through computerized leads. However, there is only one issue that an officer has the personal power to input into the lead's computer, and that is *Gang Relations*. Once an officer inputs *Gang Relations* under a suspect/offender name, it is permanent unless at a later date the officer that inputted *Gang Relations* personally removes it. The officer in question should have been absolutely positive that the suspect was a gang member before inputting such a mark. The leads system should not allow any officer to input information because it is permanent and can be used as a form of bias, retaliation or inappropriate discretion. A professional officer, upon inputting such an extreme mark on a suspect's record, would subsequently keep notes on the subject, and if the subject ten years later is an adult with children and no longer is involved in a gang, the officer will take the responsibility of removing such a mark.

Mistake 19

Ticket Quotas

Scenario 69
I gotta make my quotas tonight

I was in training, and every night my FTO *(field training officer) would remind me that I was on probation. He reminded me that I had to write at least ten parking violations per night. When I asked my* FTO *what would happen if I did not make my quota, he replied, Oh, they will find a way to get rid of you.*

The sub-culture of policing has many internal unwritten rules. For instance, ticket quotas regarding moving violations, parking ticket quotas, and arrest quotas are familiar to all law enforcement officers. Field training officers highlight ticket quotas as forms of production and promotion, and officers are reviewed accordingly. Questions arise indicative of these requirements such as: What if an officer cannot locate ten parking violations during his or her shift? What if the officer cannot find one felony arrest during the shift? What if the officer cannot make two misdemeanor arrests during the shift? Subsequent ethical dilemmas have a high probability of surfacing. The officer might have to identify innocent suspects and create factious charges to meet his or her quota. The officer might have to issue illegitimate parking tickets or moving violations. The officer might have to provoke a subject to act so that the officer can issue a commonly sought after charge such as disorderly conduct. If the officer cannot meet a departmental quota, then provoking a suspect to respond in a chargeable fashion becomes necessary. Quotas are an aggravate of corruption. Police departments should not emphasize officer arrest or ticket quotas. Professional field training officers will not enforce quotas upon new recruits. A professional officer will issue tickets and act on arrests only upon legitimate means to do so.

Federal law enforcement officers are issued cash awards for high arrest rates.

Part V

An Officer's Personal Life:
Is it really worth it?

Mistake 20

"There is only one success—to be able to spend your life in your own way."

Christopher Morley

"If a house be divided against itself, that house cannot stand."

Mark 3:25

Let it be known that what is said about men and women affects their personal and professional lives and destinations; more importantly, it affects upon how they act.

A treacherous journey for officers at times ends with difficult decisions, and much to the chagrin of officer who was prepared to aid fellow Americans shockingly has now found oneself justifying his or her career choice. The effects of the media, the job, the scrutiny, the administrative standards, and the shaky domestic lifestyle of an officer all contribute to an emotionally unsound and confused individual. The media has painted a very disturbed picture of law enforcement officials. In fact, the picture drips corruption, violence, lack of integrity, lack of honesty, and is a cancer in nature. The media does not take into account the generalized effects of its messages, which in turn demand answers from headquarters and lay heavy on the minds of officers. These malicious attacks weigh heavy on the mind of the individual officer.

The effects of heavy scrutinization from the system many times conclude in attempted suicides, aggressive behavior, and/or isolation from the outside world. What the public or the new recruit does not know is that inside the life of an officer is a very conscious world. An officer resides in a pressured world that demands low profiles, high levels of scrutiny, reaction, or no action, a steady hand or a lack thereof, reservation in front of their friends/family, an example for society, a perfect record, a perfect credit history, and an all around suspected perfect life. The pressure relating to the aforementioned is noted at the onset and throughout one's law enforcement career. An officer's world is different from many others, quietly catered to, but internally a constant battle. This world can spur emotional trauma, anxiety, and remoteness. Contemporarily the life of an officer is worsening, including even more scrutinization of officer behavior and overall demands of excellent performance. Overall excellence is concerned with one's business and personal life. How many jobs examine one's personal life? Can you imagine an interview for a secretarial position that evaluated your personal life? A police officer is surrounded by tough decision making practices, scrutinization, stressful circumstances and overall a media umbrella that encompasses poison. Critical evaluation of these surrounding circumstances before a position in the field of policing is sought is critical.

Karlberg

Scenario 70
Bad day

Upon entering work, I realized that my supervisor was distraught, quiet, and upset. He did not speak to me, so I was at a loss for assignments. The entire day he read the paper, which featured a former corrupt cop from his division who was currently on trial.

Scenario 71
The movies

The Hurricane, Training Day, Serpico, Bad Lieutenant, and Internal Affairs... movies portray officers in lives of corruption and deceit.

Scenario 72
The news

Waco, Ruby Ridge, sniper incidents, amendment violations, prison beatings, injured suspects, and overall police screw-ups are highlighted every night on television.

Scenario 73
The radio

Pigs, Bacon, 5–0 stinks, Poe Poe, shumucks, rats, narks, and fuzz are common terms featured on the radio used to describe police officers.

In the eyes of an officer, the media is responsible for society's negative perception of law enforcement. The media has portrayed the lifestyle of an officer as deceitful and violent. The media refers to television, movies, news, radio, online, newspapers, and all forms of communication technology. Disturbing television movies that portray cops as violent and malicious individuals are common. Movies that highlight corruption of officers and radio shows that coin officers as *dirty pigs* are featured regularly. The stage has always been indicative of viewing officers as threats, enemies, and the all around trader. Justifiably the officer must learn how to respond to these criticisms. The average human being is proud to announce employment status and boasts about current accomplishments. *How can an officer refer to employment status with confidence?* Take note that officers portrayed as heroes on television are few and far between. One movie is indicative of a police officer portrayed as a hero, the movie *Colors.* In fact, regularly only negative outcomes are documented. For instance, Mr. Joesph Maginowski (1991) was sentenced to life in prison. Mr. Maginowski was a former Chicago police officer whom was tasked to the ATF and who became a corrupt officer. Mr. Maginowski's case was continuously seen on television, and his face was highlighted on the front page of the paper since the onset of the incident. The incident occurred ten years prior and still haunts television, radio, and newspapers two years after the conclusion of the trial. Amazingly, the media highlights negative aspects of law enforcement and rarely reports on positive outcomes.

In the professional life of an officer, the media can dictate a positive day and/or a negative day. If an officer wakes up in the morning to an angry supervisor, a quiet supervisor, or a lackadaisical supervisor due to negative media exposure of another officer subsequently, the officer's day becomes confusing and stressful. An officer is haunted by not wanting to say the wrong thing, acknowledge the wrong issue, or speak about the negative occurrence. Therefore, tip-toeing around negative issues becomes a technique.

At the forefront of dinner conversation or at a family barbeque is an officer's personal life. Due to the fact that the media emphasizes negative occurrences, questions involving the life of an officer from loved ones are frequently subject in any conversation. Explanation is demanded even though the officer being questioned is not the officer under scrutiny. A professional officer will simply elaborate on issues highlighting the fact that not all law enforcement officers behave in a corruptive fashion and that the media exaggerates incidents. Furthermore, the media should highlight the positive accomplishments of law enforcement, which in turn will relieve stress and eventually allow an officer to be proud of identifying his or her employment status.

Mistake 21

Family Communication

Scenario 74

My second wife is leaving me, too?

When I arrive home, I don't like to speak about my negative day. My terminology has turned into street talk. Derogatory terminology has grown on me. I am always yelling, screaming, and using vulgar words. I have been a beat cop for twenty years and am not home on holidays or weekends. Everybody works on holidays, especially New Years Eve, Halloween, and the Fourth of July, but my wife does not understand. Once again, my wife is leaving me.

A police officer's home life can be very stressful. Family members have a difficult time accepting schedules and holiday workloads. It is very important to alert a prospective wife or husband on the dangers of the position, the time required, and the lack of holiday time that will be spent with the loved one. Communication indicative of the police officer's position is critical in maintaining a healthy and stable home life. The loved one needs to be reminded that the job is important, but that the family member is even more important. The family member must be understanding and in accordance with the police officer position at the onset of the relationship; otherwise divorce, break-up, and sometimes domestic violence is noted. For the police officer, communication emphasizing the requirements of the position at the onset of a relationship is essential to a stable home life.

Mistake 22

Partner Communication

Scenario 75
My partner sucks!

My partner is obnoxious and rude. He makes me feel like my night will never end. He only speaks of negative issues. My partner never breathes a positive word. Every time I attempt to speak about the positive aspects of policing, his feedback is negative.

Many seasoned officers tend to behave in a highly negative fashion. Contemporarily, a change of agenda has surfaced. Therefore, a modern professional officer will maintain positive communication. Communicating with your partner on a daily basis sometimes seems trying; however, this officer someday could save your life. Through reinforcing positive communication, an officer can begin to change the mindset of a partner to a more positive one. Jokes are a positive technique, along with positive stories about home life or the job. If a partner tends to dwell on prior negative experiences, attempt to problem solve on how the incident could have relinquished a positive outcome. A professional officer will cater to positive partner communication and will not dwell on negative experiences.

Mistake 23

Negative Energy

Scenario 76
I need to get drunk

I remember one night when I was called to the scene where a suspect had a firearm. I was the acting lieutenant that evening. I was shot at that evening. When I arrived home, I did not speak to anyone in my house. I sat quietly and drank as much alcohol as I could retain. I got so smashed that I put my fist through the wall. When I woke up for work the next day, I was hung over, late, and my wife was furious with me.

Police officers need to relieve stress after a long day's work. The negativity of the position is a constant, which results in stress for the officer. Many effects of police stress result in alcoholism, substance abuse, and sometimes even suicide. This officer should have chosen a jog after work or possibly visited his local gym to exercise. In addition, the officer needs to seek out different types of stress relievers, such as communicating with the family rather than divorcing from the family, counseling, meditation, massage therapy, music, and any means that the officer finds will compliment stress relief in a non-abusive form. Physical abuse and verbal abuse can also be effects of an officer's negative day. Divorce rates are rising for officers because a common theme of leaving one's work at the office is expected, yet difficult to accomplish. Bringing home concerns of a day's work to an understanding loved one or into a counseling type setting is a necessity, thus acts as a stress reliever. Furthermore, a successful officer on the street and at home will maintain a positive persona and will focus on positive outcomes and positive energy. In turn, the officer creates a change in mentality, which opens the floodgates to positive interactions with the community rather than negative ones.

Mistake 24

Administrative Stress

Scenario 77
The chain of command, now everybody knows

Officer Smith, a lieutenant on a different shift, always bothered me. At every meeting he would invade my space by putting his face next to mine while whispering compliments. I asked him to simply stop behaving in such a way. He refused and continued to harass me. When I told my sergeant, he told my lieutenant, and a meeting was scheduled with several other officers as witnesses. I ended up being blamed for not being capable of accepting compliments. Now the entire department was aware of the incident.

The compliments were of a sexual nature and created an uncomfortable work environment for this officer. The sergeant and the lieutenant on the officer's shift should have handled this situation privately. Instead, they alerted the entire chain of command and other officers regarding the matter, which resulted in stress for the complaining officer because of additional harassment from other officers and embarrassment. A professional supervisor would have handled the matter privately and addressed the incident with each individual rather than inviting most of the department to the meeting.

Mistake 25

Badge It, an Everyday Part of Life

Scenario 78
Bars

The cool thing about being a cop is that I can get in to any bar anytime I want without standing in line or paying a cover charge.

Scenario 79
Concerts

My friends and I had tickets to a concert, but they were nosebleed seats. They suggested that I tried badging it to move to the front row. I did, we had second row center seats the entire night.

Scenario 80
Anywhere I go

Anywhere at any time I can do whatever I want because I simply badge it!

Scenario 81
Ticket? Yeah right!

Hey, every time I get pulled over I wave my badge out the window and wait for the other officer to signal for me to keep going!

One of the perks in the personal life of an officer is carrying a badge. The badge can be used anywhere for entrance into unauthorized areas, free food, and to not receive a ticket. The badge is what most prospective officers look forward to receiving. The status symbol of the badge carries a lot of weight in any circumstance. At times a badge can be abused by the officer:

"If I do not allow this officer to sit in the front row, will he or she retaliate against me? On the other hand, if I do allow this officer to sit in the front row, maybe I will not receive any tickets." A professional officer will not use the badge in his or her personal life. A professional officer will pursue equality at all times and not seek a badge for personal gain. A potential law enforcement recruit will take note of the negative offerings of this position prior to employment. A potential law enforcement recruit will critically evaluate all aspects of the position, including mental and physical strain on the person prior to committing to employment. One must be cognizant of the negative backlash and high level of scrutiny that will be forthcoming and be able to mentally and physically endure the process.

Conclusion

A day in the life of an officer can be a wind tunnel experience. All in all, we are only human. Learn by these mistakes, and be cognizant of all of them. Start recognizing mistakes, which will begin the reconstruction of the negative perception of law enforcement that continues to loom large in the eyes of society. Cater to all the techniques listed in this text, but remember safety always comes first. Never jeopardize your safety. Believe in what you do, for you do it for others. If they seem not appreciative, you remind yourself that without you, an uncontrollable jungle will surface. Let not your emotions guide you; allow for reason, sense, ethics, and human understanding to be your guide. Never fall prey to lack of communication or hyper awareness, for you will instantaneously lose your life. Always cater to reaction, and in tense situations grasp the norm at hand. For if all these techniques are practiced, a successful law enforcement officer will be created.

References

Arrigo, Bruce, *Social Justice, Criminal Justice,* Wadsworth Publishing, 1999.

Bowie, G. Lee, *Questions In Ethics,* Harcourt Brace, 1992.

Close, Daryl, *Morality in Criminal Justice,* Wadsworth publishing, 1995.

Dempsey, *An introduction to Policing,* West, Wadsworth, 1999.

Hall, Lavinia, *Negotiation Strategies for Mutual Gain,* Sage Publications, 1993.

Harris, C. E., *Applying Moral Theories,* Wadsworth Publishing Company, 1997.

Johnson, A. Herbert, *History of Criminal Justice,* Anderson publishing, 1996.

Johnson, A. Herbert, *History of Criminal Justice,* Anderson publishing, 1996.

Krasemann, Kieth, *Questions for the Soul,* Copley publishing, 1997.

Machiavelli, Niccolo, Mansfield, Harvey, *The Prince,* University of Chicago Press, 1985.

Messner, F. Steven, *Crime and the American Dream,* Wadsworth Publishing Company, 1997.

Miller, Hess, *The Police in the Community,* Wadsworth Publishing, 2002.

More, w. Harry, *Behavioral Police Management,* Macmillian publishing Company, 1992.

Moser, K. Paul, *Human Knowledge,* Oxford University press, 1995.

Close, Meier, *Morality in Criminal Justice,* Wadsworth Publishing, 1995.

O'Brien, Maureen, *Who's got the Ball,* University Press, 1995.

Pope, Lovell, Brandl, *Voices From the field,* Wadsworth Publishing, 2001.

Rosenbaum, Lurigio, Davis, *The Prevention of Crime,* Wadsworth Publishing 1998.

17. SUN TZU, Clavell, James, *The Art of War,* Dell publishing, 1983.

Walker, Samuel, *Popular Justice,* Oxford University Press, 1998.

Walker, Samuel, *The Police In America,* McGraw Hill Inc. 1992.

Walker, Samuel, *Sense and Nonsense about Crime and Drugs,* Wadsworth Publishing, 2001.

Wrobleski, Hess, *Introduction to Law Enforcement,* Thomson, Wadsworth, 2003.

Velasquez, Manuel, *Business Ethics,* Prentice Hall, 1982.

Stojkovic, Kalinich, Klofas, *Criminal Justice Organizations,* Wadsworth, 1998.

Reece, Brandt. *Effective Human Relations,* eighth edition, Houghton Mifflin Company, 2002.